"I read this book sitting in my own 'armchair by the window' during a difficult season, and I am thankful for the honest, practical, and gentle way Everingham guides his readers. Biblically engaged, theologically robust, pastorally informed, and personally lived, this book is a gift to those who struggle with prayer in dark days. Everingham's prayer is 'that this book is a balm for your soul—a blessing, not a burden.' It has been for me."

—**KIT BARKER**, academic dean and lecturer in Old Testament, Sydney Missionary and Bible College

"In *Finding Peace through Prayer*, Mitch Everingham has gifted us with a much-needed work on the *how* of prayer. With pastoral warmth, theological nuance, and personal reflection, Everingham provides practical shape and substance to what persevering prayer looks like. Challenging, insightful, and most of all encouraging, this book is a breath of fresh air to all of us who desire to grow in prayer."

—**MALCOLM GILL**, associate minister, St. Andrew's Cathedral

"With the warmth and wisdom of a trusted friend, Mitch Everingham guides us into more intimate, effectual prayer in his new book *Finding Peace through Prayer*. Whether your prayer life feels stale or you're not sure where to start, *Finding Peace through Prayer* offers practical rhythms that can enhance all our conversations with God. This book will help you enjoy more time on your knees!"

—**CLARISSA MOLL**, author of *Beyond the Darkness: A Gentle Guide for Living with Grief and Thriving after Loss*

"It's hard to pray when times are hard and suffering is the norm. In *Finding Peace through Prayer*, Everingham offers readers a lived experience of learning to pray and commune with God through seasons of suffering. This book encouraged my soul, shaped my practice, and gave me 'confidence to draw near to the throne of grace . . . to receive mercy and find grace in our time of need' (Heb 4:16). I believe Mitch will serve you well in that endeavor also."

—**JEREMY WRITEBOL**, lead campus
pastor, Woodside Bible Church

Finding Peace through Prayer

Finding Peace through Prayer

Seven Practices for Praying in Hard Times

Mitch Everingham

WIPF & STOCK · Eugene, Oregon

FINDING PEACE THROUGH PRAYER
Seven Practices for Praying in Hard Times

Wipf & Stock
An Imprint of Wipf and Stock Publishers
199 W. 8th Ave., Suite 3
Eugene, OR 97401

www.wipfandstock.com

PAPERBACK ISBN: 978-1-6667-3870-4
HARDCOVER ISBN: 978-1-6667-9974-3
EBOOK ISBN: 978-1-6667-9975-0

11/11/22

For my parents, Jayne and Dave.
Thank you for teaching me to pray.

Contents

Acknowledgments

ABOVE ALL, I'M GRATEFUL to Jesus for his sustaining and saving grace, without which I could never have penned these words. Thank you to Suz—my wife, best friend, source of illustrations, voice of reason, and occasional editor. I wouldn't have been able to write this book without your support and prayers. To my parents: thank you for teaching me to pray and for modeling it to me. I'm eternally appreciative of you, and I thank God for you always. Ben—you're not only my brother but an unwavering friend on this journey through hard times and good ones. I'm certain that Rach would be smiling if she could see how God has grown us through our most difficult moments. A huge thank you to Ben Molyneux, Donna Kane, and James Baker for spending countless hours reviewing these chapters. Your wisdom, critique, and pastoral insights have made this book immeasurably better. Thanks also to Ellie Jacobs who provided valuable feedback on the earliest versions of these chapters, when this book was still a seed in my mind. To the faithful saints at St. Faith's Anglican Church in Narrabeen, thank you for praying for me in my own hard times. I would not be where I am today without your prayers, and I'm profoundly grateful for your example to me. Thank you also to the team at Wipf and

Acknowledgments

Stock for taking a chance on a first-time author and believing in my writing. And finally, to you—the readers of this book. I prayed for you each time I sat down to work on this book, and it fills me with joy to know you're reading this now. May you be filled with peace from our Lord Jesus Christ as you persevere in prayer.

Introduction

Searching for Peace in the Middle of a Storm

As I STARED INTO the distance, I could see the rain clouds forming on the horizon. Dark clouds of hardship and difficulty were beginning to appear, the initial glimpses of a summer storm in Sydney coming into view. And I had no plan for how to weather it.

After months of being unwell with various illnesses, countless blood tests, and an innumerable amount of days off school, I'd finally received a diagnosis: chronic fatigue. While that news certainly wasn't welcomed, I recall it so vividly for a different reason; it was the moment I realized that *life is hard.*

I'd just turned seventeen, and before you think it—yes, I probably held a little naivete to believe I could sail through life without a worry in the world. Hear me out though. Growing up on Sydney's Northern Beaches—arguably the most beautiful part of the world—life had felt as close to perfect as possible (okay, I'm a little biased . . . but seriously, google "Northern Beaches Australia"). Sure, I'd fight with my little brother and sister occasionally. And there was the first time I was dumped by a girlfriend. I'd get in trouble at school every so often (read: most weeks). Worst of all, I'd even lose my soccer games sometimes too. But aside from that— life was good. Blissful even. My parents loved me and invested in my faith, future, and friendships. They nourished the dreams I held close to my heart, even if they weren't always realistic. I found it easy to make and keep friends. I managed to have above-average grades in the classroom and to win awards on the sports field without too much effort. Our church community was like our extended family, and we spent summer days riding our bikes to the beach. It's the kind of childhood people dream about.

While there's much to be grateful for in that snapshot of my life—I recognize how blessed I was in many ways and I'm deeply thankful for that—it also meant my faith in Jesus remained uncomplicated and largely untested. I never grappled with the difficulties and complexities of life in a broken world. This meant that I knew all the theory about trusting Jesus through hardships—you pray to God for help, read your Bible, and cling to what you know to be true despite your circumstances. But in practice, I had no idea how to live that out.

It was against this backdrop that the clouds started rolling in off the horizon, and I wasn't prepared for the storm coming my way. Fast forward eighteen months from my diagnosis of chronic fatigue, and I found myself sitting in the same doctor's practice with a more confronting challenge. The previous night I'd collapsed before my Dad in tears, barely a week after stumbling through my final high school exams. The sum of my lingering sickness had amounted to a feeling so foreign that I had no other way to explain it: "Dad, I don't want to be here. I can't do this anymore."

The struggles I had endured with my physical health had begun to take such a toll on my mental health that I'd lost the desire to live. I met with a psychologist and doctor, unsure of how to chart a path upwards from what felt like rock bottom. They agreed that I had depression and needed help immediately, so with a heavy dose of reluctance, I began therapy and antidepressants. The picture in my mind of where I'd be at eighteen, the summer after graduating from school, was lying on a beach in Bali with a beer in hand. Instead, I found myself in a psychologist's office talking about how to make it to tomorrow. That's how stark the contrast felt; the gap between expectation and reality couldn't have been greater. Questions pierced with doubt began simmering in my mind: "Why isn't God hearing my prayers and making me better? Does this whole 'trusting Jesus' thing even work when life is hard? Shouldn't God be present right now, or am I expecting too much? Will I ever make it to the other side of this?"

By now, I'd worked out there were hard times in life, but I thought this run-in with suffering had surely dragged on too long. As I looked up, the clouds were thick and foreboding, hovering immediately overhead as a reminder of how much life had changed in a short space of time. And although summer in Sydney was well underway, the worst weather had yet to come.

The Eye of the Storm

When I woke on the 23rd of December, 2010, I noticed a tinge of hope creeping in; I thought that maybe I'd started to turn a corner with my physical and mental health. The previous week I'd taken a step in the right direction by returning to my part-time job after a year of being unable to work. So when my brother, Ben, and I set off for work together on our bikes that morning, there was a slight semblance of normality. A few hours into the day, as I flipped burger patties in a hot kitchen, my phone wouldn't stop ringing. I pulled it out to check who kept calling. Mum. Four missed calls. She knew I was at work—what could be so urgent? A few moments later, a family friend arrived at the counter and said Ben and I needed to leave with her right away: our younger sister Rachel had been rushed to hospital.

The moments that followed have altered my life in more ways than I will ever comprehend. Within minutes of arriving at the hospital, Rach passed away.

There was no warning or time to brace for impact. No sickness or sign that she was unwell. Only a tidal wave of shock and despair. Our flurry of questions—"Can't you do something else? Don't stop CPR! Won't it bring her back? Why didn't we know something was happening?"—was met with an answer that was no answer at all: "We're so sorry, we don't know why this happened. There's nothing we can do."

Introduction

All that the doctors could tell our family was that Rach's heart and lungs inexplicably gave way. At the age of thirteen, Rach's organs failed. And there's still no clear reason or explanation to this day. With the force of a hurricane, my family's world was turned upside down and shaken violently. The hardships I'd faced in previous years paled in an instant compared to the heartbreak that now overwhelmed me. But they also compounded. It was hurt upon hurt, grief upon grief. Rach was gone, and so was life as I'd known it.

It stung so sharply because, in lots of ways, Rach had been my best friend. I would never have admitted that beforehand—being friends with your younger sister isn't cool when you're eighteen—but it was obvious. My mates from school had given her the nickname "Mini" because they thought she was like a mini-me. We shared inside jokes, chicken burgers, and secret handshakes. I endured her ballet concerts; Rach enjoyed my soccer games. She looked up to me. I always protected her. And every night for the two years before she passed away, Rach would come into my room and pray that I'd feel better soon, even when I asked her not to. She was loving, loyal, and a beacon of light pointing me to Christ, even when I was at my most distant from him in the middle of my struggles.

I could fill a book with the story of Rach's life and death, along with the heartbreak that's followed. But I'm sure you know what I mean when I say that life became harder than I ever imagined it would. Trusting God felt almost impossible. I couldn't feel his nearness in any way. The idea of praying or reading the Bible? Forget it.

I'd love for my story to continue at this point with an event or moment where my faith immediately crystallized and strengthened as it came into contact with hardship. But the truth is, it fell off a cliff. The sharp difference between my life growing up and the one I'd found myself in felt haunting. There were two realities that I knew— a life full of goodness, peace, and joy, and one marred by death, illness, and heartache. They were like alternate universes; one was marked by what I imagined following Jesus should be like, and the other resembled a nightmare. And I had no way to reconcile them.

I'd entered the eye of the storm, and it was like no other I'd experienced. The clouds gave way to unrelenting rain, a gale blew from every side, and I was caught in the middle of it: cold and alone, soaked and shivering, unsure of where to find refuge and relief.

A Paradox We All Experience

It's worth pressing pause for a moment and asking a valid question: why am I telling you all of this? After all, you picked up a book about finding peace through prayer. Well, I wanted to begin here because I'm in the same place that you are right now: one where suffering lingers, yet a deep desire to follow Jesus remains. I live the paradox of feeling that life is both unexplainably beautiful and excruciatingly painful all at once. I've learned the hard way that looking for peace outside of Christ in times of hardship only brings more hurt. The contours of my heart contain mountain-top moments of joy alongside deep valleys of despair. And if we're honest, this is the place where most of us live—we just rarely stop to acknowledge it.

These pages are a biography of sorts, containing some of the ways I've attempted to prayerfully depend on God in the space between expectation and reality, a future hope and present hardships, the now and the not-yet. I'm someone who is clinging onto Jesus right alongside you, knowing he's trustworthy even when tears stream down our faces.

All too often our stories of ongoing pain and hardship remain untold because of our fixation with making it to "the other side" of suffering. But the reality is, that place doesn't exist in this world for many of us. We endure grief when loved ones die, agonize over the sight of sick friends, and carry the weight of living in a world that's undeniably broken. Even if my own circumstances seem to be going well at times, the longer I've lived, the more I've felt an unceasing tinge of sadness because of the injustice, suffering, and struggles that exist in the lives of those I know. We're called to bear one another's burdens, to mourn with those who mourn, and to cry out for justice on behalf of the oppressed. In this life, hardship is inescapable, not optional, because suffering is synonymous with following Jesus (2 Tim 3:12).

This book, therefore, is not a victory lap. It can't and won't give you the view that comes from standing on the other side of hardship and hurt. Instead, these chapters hold learnings from someone in the middle of the race, who longs to stay faithful to Jesus on the difficult journey we call life on this side of eternity. The truth is my heart breaks when I see the impacts of sin, suffering, and death in our world and in the lives of those I love. And I still feel the absence of Rach daily. Often my grief has a bluntness to it—like a low-grade headache that you can't shake—but other days, it feels like a part of me has been amputated, and the wound remains open. And while my physical health has graciously returned to normal, my mental health continues to ebb and flow between harder days and easier ones. This is the place I inhabit: where life is filled with very real suffering despite knowing I'm anchored to a far greater hope in Jesus. It's in this space that I've spent a decade searching for a peace that the apostle Paul promises "transcends all understanding" (Phil 4:6), a peace that can be present even in the tragedy and turmoil of life.[1]

Finding Peace through Prayer

In the moments when it feels like the world is falling apart, when you miss a loved one dearly, or illness remains a close companion—is it really possible to possess a peace that defies circumstances? And if it is, how do we find this peace that surpasses all understanding?

The purpose of this book is to answer those questions. I want us to go on a journey together where we see that this peace cannot be found in a new set of circumstances, but in the promises offered to us in Jesus and received through the practice of prayer. That claim might sound bold, or perhaps even a little too specific, but this is precisely what the apostle Paul makes clear in the book of Philippians:

> Do not be anxious about anything, but in every situation, by prayer and petition, with thanksgiving, present

---

1. Hansen, *Letter to the Philippians*, 291–92.

your requests to God. And the peace of God, which
transcends all understanding, will guard your hearts and
your minds in Christ Jesus. (Phil 4:6–7)

In these verses Paul provides us with an exhortation and a promise. The exhortation, or encouragement, is to pray to God in every
circumstance we face. And the promise is that in return we will
receive the peace of God to guard our hearts and minds in Christ
Jesus. To put it simply, praying to God results in peace from God;
one leads to the other.

This is one of the most beautiful passages in Scripture because
it shows us that God isn't interested in ignoring the realities of hurt
and hardship in our lives, and instead is concerned to provide us
with an unwavering and defiant peace in the most difficult moments we face. Through every up and down in life, the opportunity
offered to us in prayer is not one where we can always pray the rain
clouds away, but where we can always find a God-given peace in
Jesus regardless of the weather.

My hope in the coming chapters is that as we explore the
Scriptures together, this promise from Philippians 4:6–7 will lead
us to real-life practices for praying through every kind of hardship.
I'm convinced that the seven simple practices in this book will help
you to receive God's peace through prayer, and that by practicing
them you'll be reminded that your heart and mind are guarded in
Jesus no matter what comes your way. Whether you're in the midst
of trials right now, supporting loved ones who are enduring suffering, or pondering why hardships haven't yet come your way, please
know you're in good company. In many ways, this is a book written for my seventeen-year-old self—who knew some of the theory,
but none of the practice. I had no bridge between saying I would
trust God when suffering came and embodying that trust when
those difficulties inevitably arose. The practices in this book are
a guide to making that trust go from our heads to our hearts and
hands through prayer. And a little secret—thirteen years on, I need
these practices now more than ever. We all do, because experiencing suffering in this world is a matter of *when*, not *if*.

In a world marred by the uncertainties of war and disease, the countless injustices that flood our newsfeeds, and the simple daily struggles we all deal with—we can't afford to allow our circumstances to eclipse our trust in Jesus. That's why I love the words of hope that Jesus offers to his disciples in John 16, immediately after he has told them that he is going to die (John 13:33), that the world will hate those who follow him (John 15:19), and that the disciples will be scattered from one another (John 16:32);

> I have told you these things, so that in me you may have peace. In this world you will have trouble. But take heart! I have overcome the world. (John 16:33)

Jesus doesn't hide from the fact that life will be hard. He's unashamedly honest about it, so that we might turn to him and find peace. Jesus anticipates our troubles, has experienced them himself, and is with us as we face them. He doesn't ask us to bury our heads in the sand and act as if our suffering doesn't exist, because he isn't afraid of it—he has overcome the world.

I'm not sure what storms might be hovering over your life right now, but I know that life can be agonizingly hard. More importantly, Jesus does too—and he gives us permission to acknowledge that and to come to him through prayer to receive peace in return. We will have trouble, that is certain. But we can also take heart because we know the One in whom peace is found.

Seven Practices for Praying in Hard Times

We've established that there are hard times in each of our lives and that we need the peace God offers us in his son, Christ Jesus, through prayer. If that's the theory, then the rest of the book is where we get our hands dirty and learn to put this into practice. There are many books on prayer that focus on "why" to pray or "what" to pray, but this isn't one of them. Instead, we're going to work out "how" to pray on a practical level.

To do this, we'll look at seven practices for praying and consider how to implement them in our lives. I'm using the phrase "practices" to describe each of the seven practical ways to pray because I want them to be just that—practical ways of praying that we actually practice. They don't explain everything about prayer or attempt to unpack a lot of theology. Instead, they're simple, Scripture-informed models of prayer that you can implement in your life *today*.

I've found these practices to be a way of grounding myself when it feels like the earth is shaking beneath my feet. These practices are the means by which I've planted the truths I knew in my head into the soil of brokenness and mess I've found in my life and the world we live in. They've been borne out of conversations with mentors when I've wanted to run from God, through listening to the prayers of those who've suffered long before me, in reading books from saints who've lived these practices centuries ago, and by spending countless hours pastoring people in their pain. These practices have also stemmed from my own journey of seeking peace from God through prayer and searching the Scriptures for a path to navigate the struggles in my life. In a sense, the following chapters are the sum of each of those moments, and I pray they're a blessing—from one follower of Jesus to another.

None of these practices are rules or obligations; rather they're a means by which we can approach the God of peace (Rom 15:33), commune with Jesus—the Prince of Peace (Isa 9:6), and receive the peace that the Holy Spirit brings to those who believe (John 14:26–27). Consider these seven practices to be an invitation to find peace by abiding more deeply in Christ, wherever you're at in your journey. Also, don't feel the pressure to implement them all at once—that will be overwhelming and likely provide less peace than you had before! Rather see them as tools in your belt for different stages and seasons of life. I trust that over time you'll be able to incorporate each of them into your life of prayer at the appropriate times and be able to draw on them as different circumstances arise. I appreciate how author and Anglican priest Tish Harrison Warren describes this need for a variety of prayer practices:

> I've come to believe that in order to sustain faith over a lifetime, we need to learn different ways of praying.

> Prayer is a vast territory, with room for silence and
> shouting, for creativity and repetition, for original and
> received prayers, for imagination and reason.[2]

My hope is that these practices help you sustain your faith
across your lifetime by learning to pray through all circumstances,
and that they encourage you to keep holding to Jesus when it feels
like life is falling apart. I hope they're also helpful for when you're
simply having a rough day, in moments where you feel like you're
at the end of your tether, or when you're wondering where God
is in the midst of the chaos that you see on social media and the
world around you.

And my prayer is that this book is a balm for your soul—a
blessing, not a burden—no matter the storms that rage around
you. I pray it provides a way for you to know the peace of God that
transcends all understanding through prayer too.

At the end of each chapter, I'll offer a short benediction—
a prayer of blessing—as you finish absorbing the words on each
practice and reflect on what it means for your own life with Christ.

> May the following pages guide you to and guard you in Christ,
> may they point to the peace he offers through prayer,
> and may they lead to a longing to pray when life is hard.
> In the name of Jesus,
> Amen.

2. Harrison Warren, *Prayer in the Night*, 16.

Practice One

Remember the Name of Jesus

For all who pray in hard times

Growing up, I was taught to finish my prayers by saying "In Jesus' name, Amen." I knew Jesus' name was important, but I wasn't sure why I had to sign off from talking to God with the same formula every time. Was it a special incantation to make sure my prayers found their way to Jesus? Maybe it was like the genie in the bottle I'd seen in *Aladdin*, and this was the spiritual method of getting my wishes granted by God? Perhaps it all just boiled down to tradition? Each of those thoughts crossed my mind, and likely others too.

It's not an uncommon experience for many of us as followers of Jesus to mouth the words "In Jesus' name, Amen" out of routine, or because we're unconsciously repeating what we've heard others say. The problem is that we can end up reciting these words countless times and never consider the weight they hold.

As I began to ponder the purpose behind why Jesus invites us to pray these words, I realized it wasn't just a tradition or a means of getting my wishes granted. Instead, offering my prayers in the name of Jesus promised to have a profound impact by connecting me to the one who hears and answers my requests, infusing my prayers with power, and providing me with peace in the process. As we consider this first practice of prayer, remembering the name of Jesus, my hope is that you'll begin to see these same realities too.

Praying in the Name of Jesus

On the night before Jesus died, he spent time in a small upper room in Jerusalem with his disciples, teaching and preparing them for life without him. That night, Jesus offered the disciples a promise for whenever they pray in his name: "And I will do whatever you ask in my name, so that the Father may be glorified in the Son. You may ask me for anything in my name, and I will do it" (John 14:13–14).

He'll do *whatever* the disciples ask in his name. *Really?* On the surface, that sounds like a blank check for receiving anything they like (hence the genie in a bottle idea). But when we scratch below the surface, we find that Jesus is teaching the disciples—and us—something far more important and compelling. We'll circle back later in this chapter and consider whether Jesus really will give them *anything* they want, but at the core of Jesus' statement here is a greater and more fundamental declaration: he is the one who receives and answers our requests when they are offered in his name. He's reassuring the disciples that their prayers aren't received by another person or god, and they aren't filtered first for their validity by a cosmic mailman. They come directly to him.

With this claim, Jesus is making a statement that would have seemed outlandish at the time: he's claiming to hold the authority of God the Father to answer our prayers, and in doing so, Jesus declares that he too *is* God.

That might not sound revolutionary to those of us who've been Christians or around church for a long time, but to those who first heard Jesus say this—it would have made their jaws drop. To understand why, we need to rewind a little way in the biblical story and trace the theme of prayer back to its origin in Genesis 4. Cain has just killed his brother, Abel, and life outside the garden of

Eden is beginning to fall apart. Life has become hard for the whole of humanity. Evil and suffering are increasingly present. In their moment of need, where do people turn? Well, it's here that we read about the first instance of prayer in the Scriptures: "At that time, people began to call on the name of the Lord" (Gen 4:26).[1]

The one they turn to is God, and the way they turn to him is by calling upon his name—otherwise known as prayer. This is important to grasp because in ancient Near-Eastern thought, the context in which Genesis was written, calling upon the name of any god was a momentous action to take. Whenever a group of people, of any nation or religion, called upon their god, they were appealing to their entire being—their power, character, and willingness to act on behalf of their people. It wasn't offering a wishful thought or hoping that saying the name of a particular god meant their prayer would find the right recipient. Instead, calling upon the name of a god was summoning the one to whom they were praying and staking that particular god's reputation upon the response they received.

This is what we witness in Genesis as the people called on the name of the Lord—the one true God. They were asking him to act with all the power he possesses and to be true to his character and his promises.[2] It wasn't murmuring the Lord's name and crossing your fingers, hoping he might hear. It was a faithful act of praying in the name of the God they believed held the power and willingness to respond to their requests. As the Old Testament continues, this understanding of prayer becomes foundational for God's people, Israel. They understand that when they pray and call upon the name of the Lord, it is their God alone to whom they call and expect a response.

All of this sets the scene for the promise that Jesus makes in John 14 and why it was—and still is—such a profound statement. When Jesus promises to hear and respond to prayers that are offered to him, he is inviting his disciples—and us—to call exclusively upon *his* name because he is the one who God saw fit

1. Goldsworthy, *Prayer and the Knowledge of God*, 74.
2. Miller, *Praying Life*, 134–35.

to give the power and authority to hear and answer every prayer. He's reassuring all who follow him that when they pray "in Jesus' name," they are calling Jesus' character, promises, and power into action—just like Israel did with the Lord their God in the Old Testament.

The One behind the Name

One of the first questions that my wife, Suz, and I asked ourselves after we found out that we were pregnant with our first child was, What are we going to name our baby boy or girl? It's a daunting task for every parent for several reasons, not least that your child is normally stuck with whichever name you choose for life! But it's also made complex because every name has a meaning and origin behind it to consider. As we sorted through the thousands of possible names to choose from, there were a few that we managed to rule out quickly after we discovered their meaning; Kennedy, meaning "misshapen head,"[3] Cameron, meaning "bent nose,"[4] Portia, meaning "pig,"[5] and Campbell, meaning "crooked mouth."[6]

I'm sorry to all the Kennedys, Camerons, Portias, and Campbells who might be reading this book; I promise it's nothing personal. The point though is that every name has a meaning behind it, and the name of Jesus is no different. Today, when most parents choose to name their children, they pick a name they like the sound of—but for parents in the ancient world, they chose names that were aspirational for how their child would live. The meaning of a name mattered. The name "Jesus" comes from the Hebrew name Yeshua, which means "to rescue" or "to deliver," and it was given to him by God through an angel of the Lord because it was meant to point toward the salvation that he would bring (Matt 1:20–21). When God chooses the name "Jesus" for his Son,

3 "Kennedy."
4 "Cameron."
5 "Portia."
6 "Campbell."

he declared to everyone who would hear his name that this man will bring rescue, deliverance, and salvation to the world.

But you know what the most important part is? Jesus lives up to his name. He shows that he truly is the one who offers a way for people to be rescued, delivered, and saved through his perfect life, sacrificial death, bodily resurrection, and glorious ascension. This is why we read that Jesus' name is the "name that is above every name" (Phil 2:9). It's why his name is the name that we must call upon to be saved (Rom 10:13; Acts 4:12). And it's why we're invited to "repent and be baptized, every one of you, in the name of Jesus Christ for the forgiveness of your sins" (Acts 2:38). Jesus' name is more than just any ordinary name, it describes who he is, what he has done, and what he will do—or in shorthand, his character, power, and promises.

I hope it's becoming clear that when we finish our prayers by saying "in Jesus' name," we aren't just signing off correctly from our conversation with God, like putting the spiritual equivalent of an email signature at the end of our prayers. All his power—over sin, death, suffering, relationships, sickness, and life itself—is called into action when we call upon his name. His character—goodness, love, righteousness, mercy, justice, and holiness—is contained there too, because that's what we witness in his rescuing, delivering, saving work. And every promise of God finds their "yes" in the name of Jesus Christ (2 Cor 1:20). That's why we pray in his name.

Sometimes in the routine of prayer, we can often forget the One who stands behind the name in which we pray: Jesus. It can become a seemingly mundane moment when we call upon the name above every other name to act on our behalf. And the reality that we're speaking to Jesus, the one who has the power to change us, others, and our world, can even be lost on us.

I hope by now we're far enough into our journey together through this book that I can ask you a personal question: how often do you remember the significance of offering your prayers in the name of Jesus?

It's okay if it's not often. It's okay even if you'd answer "never." I freely confess that the importance of praying in Jesus' name is something I hadn't grasped for two decades of my life. But it's also a reality that has a transformative power that we desperately need. In our moments of trial and trouble, there is scarcely a truth more important for us to remain fastened to than the fact that we have direct access to Jesus, the One who can meet all our needs and answer every prayer. We pray to the sinless, crucified, risen, and ascended Lord of all things, who at this moment is seated at the right hand of God the Father in heaven, longing to hear from us and answer our prayers. Remembering the significance of praying in the name of Jesus is a perspective-shifting, peace-giving, and strength-inducing act.

Isn't it a comforting and humbling realization that Jesus invites us to pray in his name? And more than that, that he actually wants to listen to our prayers and give us what we need and what glorifies God in response? Jesus wanted us to know this, so that we would have a reassuring, confident peace that permeates the rest of our lives.

"I Will Do Whatever You Ask in My Name": The Silver Bullet for Suffering?

It's finally time to circle back to the question I danced around at the beginning of this chapter: Does this mean that Jesus will answer all our prayers exactly how we want them to be answered? It seems like he said that he would in John 14, and wouldn't that bring us peace after all? Thankfully, this offer from Jesus to hear and answer all our prayers isn't the genie in a bottle that some of us would like it to be. Instead, it means that he provides answers to our prayers that are offered in his name in a way that brings glory to God, not fleeting satisfaction for ourselves. In theory, that includes all prayers that align with what we read of the character and promises of Jesus in Scripture. In practice, Timothy Keller explains it best: "God will either give us what we ask or give us what we would have asked if we knew everything he knew."[7] That might seem unkind,

---

7. Keller, *Prayer*, 227.

but it's profoundly good news. The grace that Jesus offers us when we pray in his name is this: he will answer our prayers in a way that is for our good and the glory of his Father, not just in the way we want him to answer them. By promising to answer our prayers in this way, he extends to us the possibility of peace in our difficult circumstances. It frees us from feeling that we need to pray the perfect prayer or get everything exactly right and reassures us that we simply need to commit our prayers to Jesus and know that he has promised to hear and respond in the best way possible.

It also means that Jesus' promise isn't a blank check we can cash in to eliminate hardship and pain immediately. After all, Jesus prayed for his cup to be removed in the garden of Gethsemane, and to be spared the agony of the cross, yet God saw fit for him to endure it (Matt 26:39–42). This shouldn't deter us from praying prayers that we aren't sure align perfectly with God's will though. Instead, it means we pray every prayer in Jesus' name knowing he is good and trustworthy because he too has endured hardship and difficult answers to his own prayers.

The truth is, while we wait for the return of Jesus—when every tear will be wiped from our eyes and there will be no more mourning or crying or pain—we will experience suffering. Even if we pray. Sometimes Jesus will intervene and answer prayers in miraculous ways, and sometimes we'll scratch our heads and wonder where he is. And while the practice of remembering the name of Jesus when we pray won't always alter our situation, it does tether us to a reality beyond our circumstances. In moments of hurt and heartbreak, remembering the name of Jesus in prayer is like a salve for our wounds, lathering our trauma with the promises and goodness of a Savior who hears every word we've spoken to him. Praying "in Jesus' name" is how we feel the steadying hand of Jesus being placed on our shoulder, providing comfort and peace in the disorientation of our difficulties. And knowing the One to whom we pray anchors us to a hope beyond our circumstances, constantly reminding us of who is ruling and reigning when hardships seem to be having their way.

Friend, let me be clear. There is no silver bullet for praying away our suffering, but there is a risen Lord who knows what it's like to suffer. He still bears on his body the scars of his own death. It's this same Jesus who longs to receive and respond to every prayer offered to him when we feel bruised and broken by the tragedies of life. He is a powerful Savior who has the capacity to change circumstances. And he's also a compassionate friend who provides us with peace and comfort when life remains agonizingly hard. In both scenarios, remembering the name of Jesus and everything that it holds is where all our prayers begin and end. We're too weak, and life is simply too difficult, for us to forget the power of the One in whose name we pray.

Imagine if we were entirely conscious of Jesus' name every time we began to pray. It would not only transform the content of our prayers—it would also bring resounding peace to our souls by being mindful of the One to whom we entrust our fears, hopes, confessions, and requests.

The Practice of Remembering the Name of Jesus

In many ways, this practice is both the simplest and hardest to implement. The practice is intertwined with the theory we've walked through; knowing why we pray in Jesus' name should lead us to remember its importance and find peace simply by mouthing those words. However, because we're prone to routine and habit— which will prove to be helpful for other practices of prayer—we often remain on "auto-pilot" when we finish our prayers by saying "in Jesus's name, Amen." As a way of seeking to intentionally remember the power, promises, and character of the name in which we pray, I've offered three practical suggestions below. There's a lot of freedom in how you might choose to remind yourself of the significance of praying in the name of Jesus, but my hope is that these are a useful starting point:

Pausing

Before you begin praying, the practice of pausing and reflecting for thirty seconds on Jesus' character, promises, or words you've read that day in the Scriptures can help you to remember the beauty of praying in the name of Jesus. It also reminds you of why you pray to Jesus, and not someone or something else. Rather than remaining as an abstract entity, pausing helps to recall the One who holds the name in which you're praying before you ask him to hear and respond to your words. It also fixes your mind and heart on Jesus, transforming the inner attitude and posture that you bring into this space and in doing so, transforms the content of your prayers to align with the will of God.

Describing

When you speak the phrase "in Jesus' name, Amen" at the end of your prayer, consider describing why you're offering this prayer in Jesus' name. For example, if you're finishing a prayer where you're asking for Jesus' strength in a time of weakness, you might conclude by saying "I pray this in your name Jesus, knowing that even when I feel weak—you are strong. Amen." Taking a moment to intentionally name or describe the attributes or promises of Jesus that you need to cling to in your present hardship helps to acknowledge the power Jesus holds in this present circumstance, as well as reminding you of why you offer your prayers in his name. This practice could be taken up when you need healing from sickness, hope in hopeless situations, comfort in times of distress, and in countless other circumstances. I've often found that when I take a moment to do this, I remember why I began praying in the first place—and the tangible gift that my Savior offers in this moment.

Confessing

Often, we understand the need to confess our sin to Jesus, but what we aren't as readily aware of are our attempts to navigate our difficult journeys without him. This can be because of our self-reliance, where we trust our own abilities and strength in difficult times, or because of our forgetfulness and preoccupation with what we can see in front of us instead of being focused on Christ. In hard times, it can be helpful to explicitly confess your need for Jesus as well as confessing your self-reliance. This is similar to the practice of "describing"; however, it is more focused on reminding you of your dependency upon Jesus to hear and answer your prayers when you've become prone to self-dependency. If you find yourself in this situation, you might like to finish your prayers by saying something like, "I confess my need for you in this moment Lord Jesus, knowing that I am insufficient, but you are sufficient to meet all of my needs. I offer this in the name of Jesus, Amen."

What a wonderful name it is that Jesus holds, and what great comfort is found in knowing he is the One who receives every prayer we offer. In the next chapters, we'll turn to more specific practices for praying in the most difficult of moments, like learning to lament, but the practice of remembering the name of Jesus as you pray is intended to underpin each of the subsequent practices. My prayer is that you're refreshed and captivated by the great peace and assurance that can be found in simply recalling why you say "in Jesus' name" at the end of your prayers.

> When you pray,
> may you remember the power of the name you call upon,
> may Jesus remain true to his character and promises,
> and may you never grow weary of declaring:
> 'In Jesus' name,
> Amen.'

Learn to Lament

For when your pain is too much to bear

'GOD, I PRAY MITCH never feels sad about his sister again.'

My eyes flew open. I didn't hear another word he prayed. Instantly, my friend's words grated against every emotion I had welling up inside. A nerve had been struck, unsettling me to my core.

I'd asked for prayer moments earlier, but this wasn't what I meant. I was sad—but that was okay, wasn't it?

My thoughts hurried elsewhere. The wounds I bore were still wide open. This was jarring, like whiplash from an unexpected stop. I wore pain and sorrow on my sleeve, refusing to hide my emotions from God and others. I knew that made people uncomfortable at times—yet this moment left me completely deflated. I stood confused, two years to the day since Rach died, with hands laid on me in prayer, and began to replay countless prayers I'd heard:

> "Lord, thank you that the Everingham family know that
> Rach is in heaven and that they can rejoice."

"Thank you that Mitch has been able to move on so quickly and that life is getting back to normal."

"Father help Mitch to be strong for his family in this difficult season."

These prayers weren't the ones I wanted, nor the ones I needed. It wasn't that they were inherently wrong, more so that there was an uncomfortable disconnect: I was hurting, but most people prayed as though they wanted me to be okay right now. Questions started to swell in my mind: Is that how I should be praying too? I don't want to remove these feelings of sadness, but should I? Did God want me to put on a brave face instead of voicing my pain? Am I being unfaithful by not being outwardly "happy" or "joyful" in the face of suffering? Is the way of the faithful marked by an absence of mourning and a stiff upper lip?

I wasn't sure of the answers, but hearing my friend's prayer was the final push down a path of earnestly seeking to understand how to pray in hard times. All too often it had felt like hardship and suffering were uncomfortable problems that people wanted their prayers to solve, instead of a moment to honestly cry out to God for his help in the worst moments of life. How am I meant to pray faithfully, I wondered, when hardship is thick and hope feels desperately thin?

This is a question that afflicts every one of us. The doctor confirms your fears: the cancer has returned. Or your hope is crushed by the news of a miscarriage. For some of us, it's rising to a new day only to be met by the dark and familiar clouds of depression. You mourn the disclosure from a friend that they've been abused. Or perhaps it's arriving home to tell your family that you've lost your job; hope dims and anxiety rises. Maybe it's the toll of wars beginning, floods and fires bringing destruction, and having your newsfeed filled with the plethora of problems that plague our world. Situations like these demand our tears as much as our prayers. They're not problems to solve, but situations to grieve and circumstances to cry out to God in. Anything less is not only a failure to read the room, but it also belittles the difficulties being faced. In moments like these, how would God have us pray?

You may be as surprised as I was to learn that God has given us a model of prayer for these exact situations; the ones that hurt the most. In fact, this kind of prayer saturates large portions of the Scriptures. It's what Jesus models when he cries out from the cross, "My God, My God, why have you forsaken me?" It's a form of prayer that consumes more than 40 percent of the Psalms, as well as occupying a central place in the book of Lamentations. It's what the teacher of Ecclesiastes reminds us of when he says there is "a time to mourn" and "a time to weep" (Eccl 3:4). This type of prayer has marked the cry of believers in times of suffering throughout history, and it's a form of prayer we too need to learn.

This model of prayer is called *lament*: the honest expression of our sorrows to God. And tragically, lament has been lost from the vocabulary of many followers of Jesus today. It was absent from my prayer life, and the lives of most Christians I knew. But lament has long been the practice of the people of God when they're at the end of themselves. It's also how God himself grieved the injustices of this world when he walked among us in the person of Jesus.

Lament is a practice that we must recover. We need it desperately. When properly practiced, it provides peace for the broken and lowly by refusing to trivialize or ignore the sorrows of this life, instead offering solace in knowing that lament is also what poured from the lips of our Lord. Learning to lament is vital not only for those of us enduring hard times, but also for those longing to pray on behalf of the afflicted. The remainder of this chapter, then, has a simple but important objective: to help us learn the often-neglected practice of lament.

What is Lament?

Lament is the song we sing in the sorrows of life. Just like we wouldn't press play on a downcast and gloomy ballad as a bride walks down the aisle, we shouldn't feel the need to blast melodies of celebration when we're in the grips of despair. In the pages of

Scripture, we're repeatedly invited to sing songs that are true to life, to rejoice in times of rejoicing, and to mourn in times of mourning. In moments when it feels like it's hard to breathe, lament should be the song that rises up from our lungs.

At its core, lament is the act of verbalizing our complaints to God and calling on Him to act in response. For many of us, the prospect of "complaining" to God might sound strange, even unfaithful. But we're not talking about complaining over trivial things, like missing a parking space or there being rain on the day of a birthday party. In fact, lament and complaint are synonymous, with the act of complaining to God being presented as a faithful response in the Psalms. It's an expression of our frustration, hurt and anger at the injustice and suffering we're either enduring or witnessing—as well as a call for God to be true to his character and promises in the face of it.[1] And in the same breath, it's also a confession of trust; that God is sovereign and in control, powerful to act, and compassionate in listening to his people. Lament strikes the right chord in hard times because it expresses our deepest pain in a bold and unapologetic manner to the God who is able to hear and respond to all requests.

While there's no precise formula or rulebook on how you must lament, they often contain four distinct features. These features prove insightful in explaining how lament balances this tension of trusting God while expressing our deepest pain:

1. *Turn to God:* Prayers of lament begin by addressing God and directing the prayer toward him. The direction here is important; it's not grumbling to others—it's intentionally coming before God in prayer.

2. *Crying Out the Complaint:* This feature of lament names the problem being seen or experienced and expresses it as vividly and clearly as possible before God. This is far from unbelief or ungodliness—it's a righteous response to the wrongfulness of life's circumstances.

1. Kaiser, "Laments of Lamentation," 127–35.

3. *Appeal for God to Hear & Respond:* Here an appeal to God is made, petitioning him to be true to His character and promises. This is a way of calling for God to honor his word and his name as we saw in practice one, "Remember the Name of Jesus."

4. *Confession of Trust:* A confession of trust in God is made, acknowledging that even if the answer to the prayer is unknown, or doubt is weighing heavy, God is ultimately trustworthy despite the circumstances we find ourselves in. It's an insistence upon trusting God despite feeling the tension that our pain is standing right alongside the promises of God's goodness and mercy.[2]

This paradox is uncomfortable in a world that values certainty and clear-cut answers. For those of us who are experiencing the depths of despair in the present moment, life is likely full of complexities and disillusionment. Answers to our pain are often scarce and generally offer cold comfort if and when they do arrive. But this is precisely the space where lament is most helpful. Mark Vroegop, author of *Dark Cloud, Deep Mercy: Discovering the Grace of Lament*, explains that "lament is expressed even though the tension remains. It turns to God in prayer, vocalizes the complaint, asks boldly, and chooses to trust while uncertainty hangs in the air. Lament doesn't wait for a resolution. It gives voice to the tough questions before the final chapter is written."[3] Lament is the song that's played in hard times throughout the Scriptures, and which we'll learn to sing ourselves shortly.

Before we begin to lament for ourselves though, we're going to turn to the Scriptures to see some examples of how the song of lament is composed. While many parts of the Scriptures are beneficial for teaching us to lament—the book of Lamentations, Job and Ecclesiastes to name a few—we're focusing here on learning to lament from the book of Psalms and words of Jesus as they provide

---

2. Vroegop, *Dark Clouds, Deep Mercy,* 29.
3. Vroegop, *Dark Clouds, Deep Mercy,* 95.

us with a helpful snapshot of the diversity of laments throughout the rest of the Bible.

The Psalms and Lament

> "How long, LORD? Will you forget me forever?
> How long will you hide your face from me?
> How long must I wrestle with my thoughts
>   and day after day have sorrow in my heart?
>   How long will my enemy triumph over me?'
> Ps 13:1–2

> "My God, my God, why have you forsaken me?
>   Why are you so far from saving me,
>   so far from my cries of anguish?
> My God, I cry out by day, but you do not answer,
>   by night, but I find no rest."
> Ps 22:1–2

> "From my youth I have suffered and been close to death;
> I have borne your terrors and am in despair. . . .
> You have taken from me friend and neighbour—
> darkness is my closest friend."
> Ps 88:15, 18

These aren't exactly the faith-filled prayers many of us have been taught to pray. Questions without answers, anguish without resolution, doubt that is met only by darkness. It's grim reading. It makes us uncomfortable because it's not what we commonly hear in church services or express in our regular conversations. Are we really allowed, let alone invited and urged, to talk to God like that? Can these psalms possibly provide a pattern for our own prayers, or should they be an example of how *not* to pray?

While lament isn't only made up of voicing questions and complaints to God, it does require articulating our grievances—and yes, even validates them. And it's not a blip on the theological landscape either, a blemish on an otherwise neat and tidy book about rejoicing. Over 40 percent of the Psalms contain lament—the largest category in the Psalter.[4] Rather than these psalms being a model of unfaithfulness, they're included in Scripture as an example of how the faithful and righteous respond to the sadness and pain of life's circumstances.

In Psalm 1 we're given a vivid description of the righteous and the wicked, along with their respective paths through life. The purpose of this opening psalm is to be an invitation to the reader, that as they enter the book of Psalms they are to "identify with one or the other with the implicit message that the wicked proceed no further into the book."[5] This means that the remaining 149 psalms are words for and to those who long to live in the way of the righteous.

When I began studying theology, my Old Testament lecturer helped me understand this in a way I never had before: "God offers these words to his people as righteous responses to their sufferings and as righteous responses to the suffering of those among them."[6] Realizing this turned a lightbulb on somewhere inside me, illuminating some of the darkest and most painful crevasses of my life that I'd never known how to bring to God in prayer before. I'd spent years tiptoeing around some of the language found in the psalms of lament, unsure of whether I could pray in a similar fashion or not. But it turns out the psalms of lament weren't written to be side-stepped, puzzled over, or neglected altogether. They're included in the pages of Scripture precisely for those of us who find ourselves in similar situations, that we too might know how to respond in a way that is righteous in the face of affliction, doubt, and sorrow. The Psalms give us a model of lamenting as a gift in our suffering, a way of carrying our complaints to our Creator and lifting our songs of sorrow to his ear. It's a model that is not only sufficient for the psalmists and for us, but that Jesus himself found sufficient for his suffering too.

4. Kaiser, "The Lament of Lamentation," 127.
5. Longman III, "From Weeping to Rejoicing," 219–30.
6. Barker, "Lament as Divine Discourse," 65.

Jesus and Lament

> About three in the afternoon Jesus cried out in a loud voice, "Eli Eli, lema sabachthani?" (which means, "My God, my God, why have you forsaken me?").
> Matt 27:46

> When Jesus saw her weeping, and the Jews who had come along with her also weeping, he was deeply moved in spirit and troubled. "Where have you laid him?" he asked.
> "Come and see, Lord," they replied.
> Jesus wept.
> Then the Jews said, "See how he loved him!"
> John 11:33–36

> Going a little farther, he fell with his face to the ground and prayed, "My Father, if it is possible, may this cup be taken from me. Yet not as I will, but as you will."
> Matt 26:39

Each of these verses astounds me. Jesus knows how these stories end. He'll be raised to life after three days. He'll raise Lazarus from the dead. And his Father's will is for him to endure the cross. Yet Jesus does something profound in each of these circumstances; he remains present to the pain that surrounds him and laments that it exists. Jesus weeps with those who are weeping, and in doing so shows his nearness to the broken-hearted and grieving. He appeals to God in prayer for the suffering before him to be removed, even though it is inevitable. And then on the cross, he cries out with the words of a psalm of lament, Psalm 22: "My God, my God, why have you forsaken me?" He doesn't look for a solution to his pain or a song of praise; this is not the demonstration of faith needed in this moment. Instead, Jesus laments.

I love these passages because there's an earthiness to them. They're glimpses of Jesus as a man—the perfect God-man to be sure—but a man who is no stranger to the difficulties of life. A man of sorrows. He was, after all, betrayed by his closest friends, tortured and abused, despised and rejected, and ultimately murdered. His cry on the cross is even recorded in Aramaic, his native tongue, to demonstrate how personal this suffering was. In Jesus, we find the one person who knows all of our heartache and pain and refuses to look away from it. This is beautifully depicted in C. S. Lewis's *The Magician's Nephew*, where Digory, a little boy whose mother is sick, meets Aslan the lion. He wants to ask Aslan to help him, but he's unsure of how he will respond. Lewis writes;

> Up till then he had been looking at the Lion's great front feet and the huge claws on them; now, in his despair, he looked up at its face. What he saw surprised him as much as anything in his whole life. For the tawny face was bent down near his own and (wonder of wonders) great shining tears stood in the Lion's eyes. They were such big, bright tears compared with Digory's own that for a moment he felt as if the Lion must really be sorrier about his Mother than he was himself. "My son, my son," said Aslan. "I know. Grief is great. Only you and I in this land know that yet. Let us be good to one another."[7]

Friend, Jesus knows. He knows your deepest pain, the parts that no one else can fully understand. He grieves with you and sheds tears alongside yours. Jesus knows his resurrection is coming—and yet the perfect man laments on the cross. Jesus knows Lazarus's resurrection is coming too, and yet he weeps—God the Son takes time to grieve. We too can know the end of our stories, full of hope and heaven—a glorious resurrection—and still cry out in lament and sorrow as a righteous and faithful response to our present suffering. Jesus is good to us; he leads the way in the hardest times by modeling lament and showing us that he is with us in our lamenting. As we learn to lament, we learn to become like Christ—who validates, accepts, and embraces our suffering as real and meaningful, while simultaneously promising that in him it will one day be done away with forever. The same Savior who promises to wipe every tear from our eyes is willing to shed tears of his own alongside us as we lament. Sometimes, it seems, our peace

7. Lewis, *Magician's Nephew*, 148.

in suffering comes not from its removal but from knowing some-one is standing with us while we endure it. With that knowledge, let's now turn to take up this practice for ourselves.

Learning to Lament

In the Scriptures, prayers of lament resist being rigidly defined by a process. We can't boil them down to a formula. However, psalms of lament do contain a broad pattern for the people of God to prac-tice lament—and that's where we'll turn to learn how to lament. This pattern consists of the four features mentioned previously, and they serve as a practical and gentle guide that we can follow in seasons where the song we need to sing is one of lament. As we learn this practice of lament for ourselves, we'll use the three previ-ously mentioned psalms as our examples: Psalms 13, 22, and 88.

1. Turn to God

The first feature of lament that we need to learn is "turning to God." Psalms 13, 22, and 88 each begin by directing their prayer to God: "How long, *LORD*?" (Ps 13:1), "My *God*, my *God*, why have you forsaken me?" (Ps 22:1), and "*LORD*, you are the *God* who saves me; day and night I cry out to you" (Ps 88:1). These psalms each take up the practice from the previous chapter as the foundation for their address; calling on the name of the LORD. It's a stunning start to a lament because it indicates that God's character, prom-ises, and even his reputation is involved in their suffering—insist-ing that this is one of the places where he promises to be present and attentive to the cries of his people.

For the psalmists, they wouldn't address God if they thought he was unfaithful or unworthy of their prayers. You also wouldn't bother to pray to him if you thought he wouldn't hear you or was incapable of responding, and neither would I. The truth is, turning to God in prayer *is* an act of faith and an expression of dependence upon him in the middle of your pain. It suggests you believe he is good, just, sovereign, and merciful—or at the very least that you want to find that he is. Anyone can cry, grumble, and complain to others—only the righteous offer those cries, grumbles, and complaints as prayers to the Living God. The difference between the two is the *direction*. To lament is to believe that God is true to his word, hears the pleas of the downcast and desperate, and that he does in fact "watch over the way of the righteous" (Ps 1:6).

2. Cry Out Your Complaint

After turning to God, each of these psalms cries out with a complaint—a defining characteristic that makes them laments. In Psalm 13 this takes the form of questioning how long suffering will linger, and in Psalm 22 it intensifies to directly asking God why he has forsaken the psalmist, calling into question God's apparent inaction. Psalm 88 takes this further still, directly attributing the affliction being experienced to the hand of God with an almost unbearable cry: "You have put me in the lowest pit, in the darkest depths . . . You have taken from me my closest friends and have made me repulsive to them. I am confined and cannot escape; my eyes are dim with grief" (Ps 88:6, 8–9).

In each psalm, the extent of the complaint is laid bare before God. From the darkest depths of Psalm 88 to the lingering suffering of Psalm 13, the validity of our own cries is seen. There is no comparison of suffering or mention of someone having worse circumstances than another person. In fact, the ambiguity of Psalm 13 "allows for and anticipates a variety of future applications as the enemies are left unnamed and the exact nature of the situation remains unknown."[8] In the cries of the psalms of lament, we find voice for our own cries—no matter the situation that we face. In the depths of the pit, the moments where God seems absent, or when suffering lingers: God anticipates and hears all our cries. Psalms of lament show us that crying out our complaints with heart-wrenching honesty is not only okay but also godly. We are

8. Barker, "Lament as Divine Discourse," 55–65.

encouraged to confess our reality before God for what it truly is, not for what we wish it was.

When crying out your complaints, Stacey Gleddiesmith helpfully suggests that we remember: "a lament honestly and specifically names a situation or circumstance that is painful, wrong or unjust—in other words, a circumstance that does not align with God's character and therefore does not make sense within God's kingdom."[9] This reminds us that naming the difficulty we face is far from unbelief or ungodliness—it's a righteous response to the wrongfulness of life's circumstances. But it also provides us with a boundary for our complaints; we lament situations that are contradictory to how God has promised to act or how God intends for the world to be. For example, Psalms 13 and 22 cry out in complaint about God's absence when he has promised that he will never leave or forsake his people (Deut 31:6), and we too can cry out in complaint because we have also received this promise (Heb 13:5). Given that God intended the world to be free of all symptoms of sin, suffering, and death, it is right, valid, and necessary to lament their intrusion upon our lives or the lives of others. Once we've considered the next two features of lament, we'll look at some examples of when we can and should lament.

3. Appeal for God to Hear and Respond

Laments don't end with complaining. The third distinct feature is an appeal for God to hear and respond. This appeal holds God to his word, asking for him to listen and answer in a manner that is in keeping with his character and promises. Notice how abruptly this is expressed in Psalm 13:

> Look on me and answer, Lord my God.
>   Give light to my eyes, or I will sleep in death,
> and my enemy will say, "I have overcome him,"
>   and my foes will rejoice when I fall. (Ps 13:3–4)

---

9. Gleddiesmith, "My God, My God, Why?" lines 60–63.

There is an urgency to the request, almost like a demand: "Look on me and answer." That might unsettle us, but hear the second part of the appeal: "Lord my God." David, the writer of this psalm, knows exactly who he is talking to; and that's why he is so bold in his request. His appeal is based on an unwavering knowledge that the character and promises of God are trustworthy—even if his life circumstances provide evidence to the contrary. It is similar in Psalm 22:

> Yet you brought me out of the womb;
>> you made me trust in you, even at my mother's breast.
> From birth I was cast on you;
>> from my mother's womb you have been my God.
> Do not be far from me,
>> for trouble is near
>> and there is no one to help. (Ps 22:9–11)

In this psalm, David moves from his complaint to remembering God's character and prior faithfulness to him (9–10), before making his appeal for God to "not be far". There is a logical progression from the problem being faced to finding solace in God—showing us that "his complaints are not cul-de-sacs of sorrow but bridges that lead him to God's character."[10] Even in the darkness of Psalm 88, the psalmist acknowledges "Lord, you are the God who saves me" as the opening posture of the psalm, before appealing for God to hear—"May my prayer come before you; turn your ear to my cry" (Ps 88:1–2).

As people living after Jesus' death and resurrection, our prayers of lament are now anchored in what we believe and know to be true about the character and promises of God revealed to us in Christ. We can know of God's faithfulness to save us and meet us in the depths of our cries even more than the writers of the Psalms. This is why the author of the book of Hebrews writes:

> Therefore, since we have a great high priest who has ascended into heaven, Jesus the Son of God, let us hold firmly to the faith we profess. For we do not have a high

10. Vroegop, *Dark Clouds, Deep Mercy,* 58.

priest who is unable to empathize with our weaknesses, but we have one who has been tempted in every way, just as we are—yet he did not sin. Let us then approach God's throne of grace with confidence, so that we may receive mercy and find grace to help us in our time of need. (Heb 4:14–16)

Jesus, the one who sits upon a throne of grace in heaven, knows what it's like to experience weakness, to suffer, and to be tempted. He's the one to whom we pray, and who pours out mercy and grace in response. What confidence that should provide us with in our moments of despair.

4. Confess Your Trust

Finally, laments generally finish with a confession of trust or vow of praise. I say "generally" because they don't always make it there. This final movement in prayers of lament is a way of expressing trust in God even if the answer to your prayer is unknown, doubt remains heavy, or suffering is ever-present. It's a confession that God is still praiseworthy even when pain feels more present than his promises.

In Psalm 13, David closes with the confession: "But I trust in your unfailing love; my heart rejoices in your salvation. I will sing the Lord's praise, for he has been good to me." (Ps 13:5–6). David acknowledges that despite his current circumstances, God's love never fails, and he will continue to place his trust in God and offer him praise. Note that his reality isn't altered—the word "but" highlights the paradox of this—and the tension continues to linger in the air. It doesn't erase that he feels forgotten (Ps 13:1); he simply confesses that he will continue to trust despite his feelings. It's similar in Psalm 22, where David again confesses, "I will declare your name to my people; in the assembly I will praise you" (Ps 22:22), even while asking to be rescued "from the mouth of the lions" in the previous verse (Ps 22:21). An immediate resolution is not found, but it doesn't stop David from declaring that God is trustworthy. David knows God's track record, so he is willing to confess his trust. It's a posture of expressing faith amid doubt, of being rooted in trust while continuing to cry out with complaints, and depending upon God's promises even while acknowledging that pain is real.

While both Psalms 13 and 22 close with confessing their trust, Psalm 88 takes up another note: "You have taken from me friend and neighbour—darkness is my closest friend" (Ps 88:18). The tune played here is more harrowing, and the depths of suffering are evidently deeper. And yet while the psalmist cannot bring themselves to declare praise as the climax of their song, they have expressed their trust in God already by addressing the God who can save them in the opening verse. Geoff Harper explains that "this psalm allows, even encourages, us to name things for being as bad as they are . . . Ps 88 demonstrates that expressing grief, even anger, to God is not an immature or unspiritual thing to do; it is not a slippery slope towards atheism. Rather, to lament is a righteous act carried out in full assurance of faith."[11] Even in the darkest, hardest, and most painful circumstances of life—when speaking words of trust and declaring praise is too much to bear— lamenting is always an act of faith and a confession of trust in God.

Practicing Lament: An Honest and Uncomfortable Path to Peace

It can be hard to know where to begin when it comes to practicing lament, and how to move from words on a page to praying in real life. In his book *Lament for a Son*, the Christian philosopher Nicholas Wolterstorff gives us a vivid and helpful image into how we practice lament:

> But please: Don't say it's not really so bad. Because it is. . . . If you think your task as comforter is to tell me that really, all things considered, it's not so bad, you do not sit with me in my grief but place yourself off in the distance away from me. Over there, you are of no help. What I need to hear from you is that you recognize how

11. Harper, "Lament and the Sovereignty of God," 80–93.

painful it is. I need to hear from you that you are with me in my desperation. To comfort me, you have to come close. Come sit beside me on my mourning bench.[12]

When we lament, Jesus sits beside us on our mourning bench. He knows what it is like, even if no one else does, because he too has lamented. Lament is also how we sit on the mourning bench that belongs to others who suffer. I didn't know it at the time, but a prayer of lament was what I needed from my friend who asked God to help me "never feel sad again." I'm sure he prayed for me in the best way he knew how to—I think most people pray as faithfully as they can with the tools they've been given. The purpose of this chapter isn't to critique, but to provide a more biblical, faithful and Christ-like way to pray in the difficulties of life. It's adding another tool to your belt of prayer in the form of lament.

The beauty of learning to lament is that it offers a way to name the uncomfortable realities we face with unflinching honesty before God, all the while defiantly clinging to his goodness and promises in Christ. Embracing that tension, I believe, is why lament offers us a path to peace. It refuses to ask us to lift our chin, grit our teeth, and solider on. It doesn't minimize our difficulties or water down our worries but fixes our sights on what is true; life is momentarily hard, God is eternally good, and acknowledging both realities is necessary. Lament invites us to "live in harmony with what is real" and reminds us that God is comfortable with our questions and complaints even when we aren't.[13]

To conclude this practice, here are four suggestions I want to offer you as a way of beginning to lament for yourself, and learning to sit on the mourning bench with others:

Lament Every Hardship

It's true that lament provides us with language for the lowest moments in life, but it would be wrong to assume lament is only for

12. Wolterstorff, *Lament for a Son*, 34.
13. Patston, "Lament and Pastoral Care," 237–48.

the worst of times. If God longs to make all things right in the new creation, it is appropriate to lament any and every hardship, no matter how insignificant we perceive them to be. This could be things like the flu, a lost job, or unfulfilled dreams—because they're all intrusions on how God intended his world to be. Learning to lament these circumstances will also form us into competent lamenters in the darker valleys of despair that will inevitably come our way; or the way of those we know. In each instance of sorrow, whether they are big or small in our minds, we can turn to God, cry out our complaints, appeal for him to hear and respond, and confess our trust in him.

Lament for Others

Part of the gift of this practice is that it provides a way for us to pray on behalf of others. To lament is not only to partner with the crucified Jesus in crying out "My God, My God, why have you forsaken me?" but also to ask God why he has seemingly forsaken others and the world which we inhabit. It's how we pray for those who are in tears, stand in solidarity with those who mourn, fight the injustices we see by calling on God to act, express our disdain and anger at the corruption of this world, and continue to be a faithful witness when life is falling apart around us. Paul Miller, the author of *A Praying Life*, helpfully explains that "there is no such thing as a lament-free life. In fact, if your life is lament-free, you aren't loving well. To love is to lament, to let your heart be broken by something."[14] Lamenting for others is an act of love, not because we've provided a solution to their pain, but because we've entered it with them.

Befriend the Psalms

At best, the four features of lament I've outlined in this chapter are a simple guide to lamenting. However, the most helpful guide you

14. Miller, *Praying Life*, 173.

can learn from is the Psalms because not only are they a model of how to lament; they're also a companion in your hardship. Befriending the psalms of lament will allow you to learn from fellow believers who've walked the well-worn path of suffering ahead of you and faithfully cried out to God along the way. You can even pray these psalms as your own prayers by interjecting your specific circumstances and complaints, and in doing so you'll learn the art of lamenting more thoroughly than this chapter could ever explain.

Write Your Laments

You might like to practice writing your own lament using the four features outlined in this chapter, or by modeling a prayer from a particular psalm that resonates with your present situation. The act of writing your prayers often brings clarity to the words you're seeking to bring before God, as well as solidarity with the writers of Scripture as you model your prayers after theirs.

My prayer is that you find that the peace of Christ guards your heart and mind through learning to lament, and that you and others find solidarity with your Savior who himself modeled lament.

> May you turn to God regularly through lament,
> to cry out your complaints and on behalf of others,
> to appeal for God to hear and respond,
> and to confess your trust in the One who invites us to lament.
> And may God in turn grant you peace,
> through this honest and uncomfortable form of faithfulness.
> In Jesus' name,
> Amen.

PRACTICE THREE

Embrace Silence

For when words are too hard to find

"I HAVE OFTEN SAID that the sole cause of man's unhappiness is that he does not know how to stay quietly in his room."[1]

That's the conclusion that the French philosopher Blaise Pascal arrived at. It's certainly a bold statement, but here's the scary part: this was Pascal's observation in the 1600s. Long before smartphones and the internet hijacked our attention, humanity began to shift from embracing time alone in silence to rejecting it.

Pascal might be exaggerating—there are certainly problems caused for other reasons—but he's got a point. We don't like silence. In a fast-paced and noisy world, turning the volume down to zero feels jarring and unnatural. As life progresses, most of us turn the volume up by taking on more roles and responsibilities while we cram as much as we can into our finite existence. We're often uncomfortable with being in a truly quiet space or state. We can be afraid of what comes out in the silence of our lives, especially

1. Pascal, *Pensées*, 118.

in hard times. It forces us to confront the realities deep within us that would otherwise lay unaddressed, gathering cobwebs and dust. Instead, we're prone to choosing avoidance, entertainment, and distraction as a way of numbing our inner pain and neglecting how we truly feel.

Journalist Andrew Sullivan discovered this problem first-hand when he decided to break his self-professed "addiction" to technology and social media and replace it with silence. Embarking on a ten-day silent retreat with no access to his phone, social media, the internet, or even verbal conversation with another human being—Sullivan came undone. In his *New York Magazine* article titled "I Used to Be a Human Being," he details the pain of his childhood that came bubbling to the surface after only a few days of silence. The trauma of witnessing his mother struggle with mental illness only presented itself decades later, which wasn't at all what he anticipated experiencing during this time: "It was as if, having slowly and progressively removed every distraction from my life, I was suddenly faced with what I had been distracting myself from. Resting for a moment against the trunk of a tree, I stopped, and suddenly found myself bent over, convulsed with the newly present pain, sobbing."[2] In the absence of noise, Sullivan's pain rose to the surface. There was nowhere else to go.

Perhaps his most striking reflection though is about what happened over the next several days: "The sadness shifted into a kind of calm and rest. I felt other things from my childhood—the beauty of the forests, the joy of friends, the support of my sister, the love of my maternal grandmother. Yes, I prayed, and prayed for relief."[3] While Andrew Sullivan is skeptical that prayer was the pivotal ingredient that shifted his pain to peace, we'll discover in this chapter that his embrace of silence may have been closer to prayer than he could have imagined.

The practice of "embracing silence" in prayer is one where we intentionally come before God in silent, wordless prayer. In a world full of noise, this is perhaps the most counter-cultural

2. Sullivan, "I Used to Be a Human Being."
3. Sullivan, "I Used to Be a Human Being."

practice in this book. But if we truly want to allow Jesus to guard our hearts and minds, we need to learn to quiet our lives before God in prayer. Embracing silence is for those who have no words in the difficulties of life, and, as we'll see, it's often the place where the most powerful prayers are offered to God and where peace that transcends all understanding is found.

I understand that it might sound like the opposite of faith to pray without words, so before we begin, I want to give you a roadmap for this chapter. First, we'll look at the example of Jesus who regularly went to a silent place to pray. While Jesus didn't necessarily pray without words, we'll see in the second section of this chapter that Jesus' practice of seeking external silence led to many believers throughout church history embracing silent, word-less prayer as a way of internalizing what their Savior modeled. Then we'll turn to Rom 8 and see the biblical basis for this practice, noticing that in our hardest moments, when words are too difficult to find, the Holy Spirit is in fact praying already on our behalf. To conclude, we'll bring together the examples we've considered and the knowledge that the Spirit prays for us into a simple practice for embracing silence before God as a form of prayer.

Our Savior in the Silence

Throughout the Four Gospels, we're repeatedly told that "Jesus often withdrew to lonely places and prayed" (Luke 5:16). It's an inescapable pattern throughout Jesus' life and ministry. The word used for "lonely places" is the Greek word *eremos*, which can be translated in a range of ways: wilderness, a solitary place, a desert place, or a quiet place.[4] While there are many translations, they all describe the same physical setting: a place that was intentionally away from other people and distractions where silence could be found. What does Jesus do in these quiet places? He prays, and he does so often.

---

4. Comer, *Ruthless Elimination of Hurry,* 123–24.

We see this in the Gospel of Mark, which begins with a brief account of Jesus' baptism before immediately shifting focus to his time in the *eremos*. Jesus spends forty days out in the wilderness, removed from everything other than wild animals, angels, and the temptation of Satan. He then returns to Capernaum for a few days to preach the gospel, call people to follow him, and heal many. After these long days of ministry, what does Jesus do? Put his feet up and relax? Take a day at the beach by the shores of the Sea of Galilee? Indulge in a long dinner with friends? Nope. He wakes up "very early in the morning," forsaking sleep, and heads straight back to "a solitary place" to pray (Mark 1:9–35).[5]

Who does that? Most of us struggle immensely with times of silence and isolation. We reach for our phone as soon as no one is around and begin to mindlessly scroll. We even find it difficult to spend five or ten minutes alone with God each day. Jesus, on the other hand, seems utterly dependent upon having times of silence alone with his Father. And get this: the only reason Jesus returned to civilization in the middle of Mark's account wasn't because he got bored of spending time praying alone; it was because the disciples sent a search party to find him and bring him back to Capernaum.

Perhaps the most important detail to consider for our purposes of learning to pray in hard times is that Jesus often withdraws to the *eremos* when life is most difficult. Before Jesus chooses the twelve disciples—one of the most significant decisions throughout his earthly life—he withdraws to a mountainside alone to pray (Luke 6:12). After hearing of the death of John the Baptist, his friend and the one who prepared the way for Jesus to come, we find our Savior taking a boat to a solitary place (Matt 14:13). In that moment of grief, the place that Jesus turns is not publicly denouncing Herod for murdering his friend—but silence. Where is Jesus when he's tempted by Satan? In the *eremos* (Mark 1:12–13). How does Jesus process difficult days of ministry, like driving demons out of people? By going to a solitary place (Luke 4:42). And the pinnacle of these examples comes in the garden of Gethsemane, when Jesus' "soul is overwhelmed with sorrow to the

---

5. Comer, *Ruthless Elimination of Hurry,* 125–26.

point of death," and he retreats to pray alone not once—but three times (Matt 26:36–44). When life is at its worst for Jesus, he goes to a solitary place to pray. The pattern is unavoidable.

Think about that rhythm of life for a moment; the Son of God intentionally made time to sit in isolation and be with his Father in prayer. Even Jesus needed to be alone, embracing silence, and praying in a space away from the difficulties and distractions of life. How much more should we be doing so in our times of hardship?

It doesn't mean we have to retreat to the literal wilderness— it could be an armchair by the window, a park or beach nearby, or the kitchen table once the kids have gone to bed. But if Jesus modeled this kind of prayer life, we'd be crazy to think that we can go without it.

Looking at the example of Jesus in the Gospels only gets us so far though: in this chapter I'm encouraging us to embrace silent, wordless prayer before God—and we can't possibly know if Jesus did this or not. It's a detail the Gospel writers either don't know or don't record for us. What we do know, however, is that Jesus was serious about having a silent external environment. And for the last two millennia, faithful saints have looked at this example from Jesus and seen it as a reason to quiet their inner life of prayer before God too.

The (Almost) Silent Testimony of Faithful Saints

While we might be reluctant to embrace times of silence today, this hasn't always been the case for followers of Jesus. Since the time of the early church, Christians have frequently embraced the practice of silent, wordless prayer before God. Allow me to take you on a highlights tour of this practice throughout church history to help us see this together.

In the third and fourth centuries there was a relatively little-known group of men and women known as the "desert fathers and mothers." As they looked on at the corrupt and compromised Christianity that they saw in their culture, they decided to retreat to the desert to grow in Christlikeness and to devote their lives to prayer. During this time one of the most well-known desert fathers, Anthony of the Desert, said this about prayer: "Wherever you go, keep God in mind; whatever you do, follow the example of Holy Scripture; wherever you are, stay there and do not move away in a hurry."[6] Did you notice how little he says about using our words to pray? He encourages attentiveness to God and unhurried prayer that was modeled on the Scriptures, but not speaking. A contemporary of Anthony who went by the name Abba Moses similarly encouraged a disciple who sought his counsel to "Go and sit in your cell, and your cell will teach you everything."[7] Silence was viewed by Abba Moses as a formative and vital way of being with God and learning from him. And then we get the testimony of the great Augustine of Hippo, commonly known today as Saint Augustine, who wrote shortly afterwards: "Why do you want to speak and not want to listen? You are always rushing out of doors but are unwilling to return into your own house. Your teacher is within."[8] There was something about ceasing to speak and embracing silence that was vital to these early church leaders as they pursued a life of prayer. For them, prayer was about far more than offering our words; it was about stopping to be silent and listen before God.

If I'm honest, silent prayer has puzzled me for a long time (and sometimes still does). Normally when I have a moment to myself, I find my mind running in a million different directions—or wanting to switch off mentally and turn on the TV instead. I look back on these early saints and find their practice kind of, well, weird. If their testimony weren't preserved in written form, I would scarcely believe they valued silence so highly that they fled to a desert to pursue it. Maybe it just doesn't compute well in my extroverted, can't-sit-still, million-miles-an-hour brain. I've even wondered before if this practice of silence was simply a cultural norm in antiquity, an old-school way of showing reverence, and times have changed a little too much now to pick this practice up again.

6. Greig, *How to Pray*, 58.

7. Sittser, *Water from a Deep Well*, 83.

8. Augustine, *Exposition of the Psalms*, 297.

However, as I puzzled over some of these ancient figures during my time in theological college, I realized that this embrace of times alone in silence continued to be practiced by more recent saints too. Dietrich Bonhoeffer, the German pastor and martyr who lived during the Second World War, said: "We are silent early in the morning because God should have the first word, and we are silent before going to bed because the last word also belongs to God."[9] This is from a man who was murdered for his faith during the worst war of modern times. He had every reason to cry to out to God for help. But what was his practice? Silent, wordless prayer before God every morning and evening—even when life was unimaginably hard.

Brother Lawrence, the seventeenth-century monk and author of the classic work *The Practice of the Presence of God*, also embraced silence. Having grown up in poverty before being forced to retire prematurely from the army with a crippling injury, Brother Lawrence knew suffering and difficulty. These experiences led him to describe his prayer life in this way: "I call this the actual presence of God. It is a habitual, silent, and secret communion of the soul with God."[10] Brother Lawrence, Bonhoeffer, the desert fathers and mothers, and countless other followers of Jesus throughout history have a common thread to their prayers; they often prayed not with words—but with silence. They internalized Jesus' external commitment to praying in a silent place. Why? Because this is the place where they believed God was present and, somehow, where God also spoke.

If you're like me, there are still a few questions that you need answered about this form of prayer. Perhaps your pragmatic side is wondering, How can silence be a form of prayer? It's a good question, because almost all Christians have been raised to understand prayer as offering words to God. Or maybe your theological background makes you pause and say, "This seems a little left field; what do you mean God can speak when we are silent? Where's the biblical precedent for this?"

9. Bonhoeffer, *Life Together*, 85.
10. Brother Lawrence, *Practice of the Presence of God*, 20.

I hear your questions. I've had them too. And answering these questions is the final piece of the puzzle that we need to put into place before we take up this practice of silent prayer for ourselves.

The Spirit Intercedes in the Silence

To find the answers to our questions, we need to turn to Romans 8. It's a chapter of the Bible that reveals countless beautiful truths, like the promise that God will work for the good of those who love him in all circumstances, and that we are called children of God through Jesus' death and resurrection. While these are wonderful realities, the apostle Paul is writing them to believers in a specific set of circumstances; they're enduring hardship and suffering (Rom 8:18–25). And Paul's aim is to encourage them to have hopeful trust in the goodness of God and the promise of salvation despite their circumstances. It's in this context that he records for them, and for us, one of the most astonishing promises in Scripture:

> In the same way, the Spirit helps us in our weakness. We do not know what we ought to pray for, but the Spirit himself intercedes for us through wordless groans. And he who searches our hearts knows the mind of the Spirit, because the Spirit intercedes for God's people in accordance with the will of God. (Rom 8:26–27)

Take this promise to heart: When you feel weak or when you don't know what to pray, the Spirit of the living God intercedes and prays on your behalf. When life is too much to bear and the circumstances you face cause you to groan with sadness or helplessness, there is a helper who prays for you through wordless groans. In seasons of suffering and when hope seems like a distant possibility, the Holy Spirit speaks to God with words we will never fully comprehend. We don't even need to ask—he knows that we need his help, and he begins to intercede for us. And he doesn't just offer any old prayer; he prays in accordance with God's will—the kind of prayer that God urges us to pray and that he promises to answer.

Have you ever pondered how incredible this truth is? The God who loves you, sent his Son for you, and now calls you his child has also made it clear that the Holy Spirit prays for you when your circumstances make it too difficult to utter words. It's not only astounding to think about, but it also offers us deep peace in the darkest of moments. As Tish Harrison Warren says, "In our long, dark nights we don't know how to pray. But we know God, the one who prays for us. And that is enough."[11] In your suffering and speechlessness, dialogue between God the Father and God the Holy Spirit is taking place. In our silence, the Spirit speaks.

We don't always need to offer words in order to pray. This is what the desert fathers were speaking of, and why Bonhoeffer advocated for silent prayer to begin and end the day. We also don't need to utter words if they are too hard to come by. Instead, we simply need to be present to the conversation that is already happening. We can trust that the Spirit is making petitions on our behalf and in line with God's will; and that is prayer as much as when we use our words.

I'm sure you know the experience of struggling to find the right words to pray. I've been in that situation countless times, from days when my mental health makes it hard to even get out of bed, to moments when my grief is particularly painful. It's normal that we don't know what to pray sometimes. Romans 8:26–27 is a source of hope to each of us who face those moments. It reassures us, as Tim Keller says, that "it almost seems that the help of the Spirit is triggered by our helplessness."[12] There is great comfort to be found in recognizing that God doesn't require eloquently articulated prayers, but a recognition that we are weak and in need of help. In fact, this is precisely the place that our helper, the Holy Spirit, inhabits with his prayers.

Our problem though, is that we often don't stop for long enough to recognize this is happening. In our desire to resolve the problem of suffering we rush to speak to God with words. But embracing silence is equally necessary—sometimes more

11. Harrison Warren, *Prayer in the Night*, 111–12.
12. Keller, *Prayer*, 132.

so—because the same Spirit who empowered the ministry of Jesus and raised him from the dead is speaking to God on our behalf. What if our greatest need is to acknowledge our weakness and sit silently before God, knowing the Spirit is interceding for us? What if we consciously took the time to become aware that the Spirit is praying for us when we don't what to pray, instead of burdening ourselves with finding the right words? And what if embracing silence—alone in a room, on a quiet beach, or walking in a forest—holds the possibility for us to join in on praying the prayers we most desperately need to pray? This is what Jesus and the saints who've gone before us all seemed to know and rely on in hard times. And it's a practice that we would do well to recover.

I'm not sure what grief is present in your life right now, what hurts you're carrying with you, or the challenges that your current season holds. But I do know this: the Holy Spirit knows your weaknesses. And when you don't know what to pray—he intercedes for you in accordance with God's will, so that all things in your life would be worked together for your good in Christ (Rom 8:27–28). When it's hard to pray or words are too difficult to form, you can find peace in this promise by simply realizing that your silence is prayer.

Embracing Silence

If our purpose in this book is to find peace in the difficulties of life through prayer, then it seems the practice of silent prayer is one we cannot afford to neglect. Pastor and author A. J. Sherill said this about silent, contemplative prayer: "That this form of prayer has been elusive in the Western church is a tragedy. So many of our spiritual ancestors were committed to this pathway of following Jesus. Maybe we should follow their lead—as they followed Christ."[13] The good news is, we can follow their lead. Having seen the breadth of historical practice from the life of Jesus and many saints throughout the centuries, we're now ready to embrace silence

13. Sherill, *Being with God*, 34.

too. I've offered four simple steps that will help with implementing this form of prayer in your life today, as well as a simple prayer you might like to pray when you begin a time of silent prayer (ironic, I know).

1: Name Your Silence "Prayer"

Begin by naming your silence before God as "prayer." Given that much of our understanding of prayer revolves around the words we speak to God, it can be helpful to proactively identify the practice we're engaging in as "prayer." This isn't for God's benefit, because he knows our hearts already, and the Spirit intercedes for us without our prompting. Rather, it's for our own recognition of the space we are entering, designating our posture before God as one of prayer. It also helps us to be intentional, marking our silence as sacred and our sighs as set apart for God amidst the difficulties of life. It's important for us to name our struggle to pray, knowing that this where the Spirit intercedes, and to recognize that our groaning can be godly. Taking the time to identify this truth is often the most helpful place to start.

2: Focus on Relationship

In times of sorrow and suffering, the greatest comfort we can find is often simply being in the presence of people who understand how we feel without needing to explain ourselves. We also cherish the company of the person who doesn't need to offer words because a compassionate look, a warm embrace, or sitting silently next to each other is all that needs to be said. This I how I understand silent prayer before God; he knows my heart and mind before I come to him. He sees my sorrow and anguish. He knows my greatest needs without me needing to express them. Instead of offering words, I'm able to rest in the knowledge that Jesus is my great intercessor who made a way to know God (Heb 7:25), the Spirit is praying on my behalf (Rom 8:27), and my relationship with God is eternal and secure (John 3:16). I can focus on the relationship I have with the Triune God, no matter the circumstance I face, and find peace by resting in that reality.

Pastor and author Rich Villodas describes it like this: "In basic terms, silent prayer is the practice of focusing our attention upon God through the simplicity of shared presence. It's a surrender of our words to be present with the Word (with Jesus) . . . silent prayer focuses on relationship, not words and speaking."[14] This mirrors the encouragement of the psalmist to be still before God and direct our focus to his character, promises, and goodness (Ps 46:10). In silent prayer, we focus on the One to whom we come, not what we'll say when we arrive. And on a practical level, it means we know what our minds should be occupied with when we're not focusing on speaking!

3: Start Small

Allow yourself the grace to start small if this prayer practice is new to you. At first, it might feel strange or uncomfortable to be silent for more than a few moments. In today's world, we aren't conditioned to open ourselves in a vulnerable way, and entering a space of silent prayer before God might uncover deep wounds. Starting with a few minutes of silence and being gentle as you begin this practice is more than okay. It's also normal to find it difficult to quiet your mind and heart before God—our world is full of non-stop noise after all. I've spoken to a lot of people who've felt that in theory, it shouldn't be that difficult to offer silence before God as a prayer; but in practice, it's been hard to implement.

A helpful practice as you begin is to set a five-minute timer, which serves as a way of focusing your time and providing a helpful limit. Sometimes we want to dive in deeper and commit to a new practice as wholeheartedly as possible, but I'd encourage you to slowly wade into the waters of silent prayer. This will help to avoid feeling frustrated if you find it difficult to remain focused at first, as well as being gentle in laying bare the difficulties of your life before God. Remember: silence is like a foreign language

14. Villodas, *Deeply Formed Life*, 23.

in our world. It takes time to become accustomed to this. Begin slowly, trusting that this practice will bear fruit in accordance with God's will over time.

4: Find Your *Eremos*

At the beginning of this chapter, we thought about Jesus' practice of going to the *eremos*; a solitary place, desert place, wilderness, or a quiet place. You might not have a desert nearby, but you probably have an armchair at home to sit in with your morning coffee, that park around the corner where you can sit under a tree, a nearby beach that calms your soul, or a few moments each night when the house is silent, and you can sit alone on the couch. Wherever it is—find your *eremos*. Identify the place where you feel at peace and can be alone and silent before God, and then create space in your life to leave the noise and distractions behind so that you can enter your *eremos* regularly—even if it's only for five or ten minutes. This is also a helpful way of linking your inner posture of silence before God with an external environment that is quiet.

If you're like me, your phone is probably going to be your greatest distraction. I've had to become disciplined in turning it off or leaving it behind altogether and bringing along a journal and a pen instead. When thoughts arise that distract you, or you have a lightbulb moment during prayer where something suddenly makes sense, you can stop to write them down in a journal and not worry about forgetting them.

As you enter a time of silent prayer, here is a short prayer that you might like to pray:

> Father,
> I feel weak as I come before your throne of grace today.
> I simply don't have words to offer.
> Hear my silence, Lord,
> and remind me of the divine dialogue already taking place.
> Thank you that the Spirit intercedes now on my behalf,
> because of Jesus, my great intercessor.
> In Jesus' name,
> Amen.

Peace When Words Are Hard to Find

The wise teacher of Ecclesiastes reminds us that "there is a time to be silent, and a time to speak" (Eccl 3:7). I hope it's been clear in this book already that there are innumerable moments where it is vital to speak to God in prayer when we're navigating hard times. The purpose of this chapter, however, has been to draw attention to a blind spot in many of our prayer lives: the importance of moments when it is time to be silent in prayer. Not only is this practice biblical and historical, but it is also essential for followers of Jesus today to recapture silent prayer as a means of finding the peace that Jesus offers us.

I know this practice might feel strange to begin with. But I also know it's following the way of Jesus—the way of peace in hardship and comfort in crisis. What greater peace could be offered to us amid our sorrow and suffering than knowing that the Holy Spirit is interceding on our behalf when words are too difficult for us to find?

In your groaning and your grieving, your inability to find words and your times of weakness—embrace silence. And know that this silence is prayer, because the Spirit is already present—praying with and for you in accordance with the will of God.

> May you find freedom from needing to find the right words,
> and instead find peace in offering your silence before God—
> knowing that the Spirit intercedes in your weakness,
> and prays in the will of God on your behalf.
> In Jesus' name,
> Amen.

Pray the Scriptures

For when you're searching for the right words to pray

HAVE YOU EVER HAD one of those moments where you want to pray for someone, but you just don't know what to pray for? What about a season in life where you've longed to express yourself to God with words, but they've simply felt too hard to find?

One night as I sat down at the dinner table for a meal with my family, I found out that my grandfather had received a devastating diagnosis: terminal cancer. Immediately, I wanted to turn toward him and pray; but what on earth was I meant to say in this situation?

In another season of my life, depression held a tight grip on me, and I found it a struggle to even make it out of bed most days. I wanted to cling even tighter to Jesus in this moment, but I had no idea what to pray. Where can we find words when we're in the depths of despair?

Only a few years ago, I walked into my uncle's house just days after my aunty had passed away. My chest became tight at the thought of praying with my cousins and uncle. I longed to offer words of comfort and peace in their time of grief, but how could I possibly conjure up the right words in such a situation?

In each of the situations, I've been at a loss for words. I wanted to pray but trying to find the words to express myself proved elusive. It often felt like grasping at thin air as I tried to make sense of the circumstances or offer some kind of comfort and hope in response.

We all have those experiences at times, where words feel too difficult to summon, linger just out of reach, or come to mind after the situation has passed. And not only when we pray for ourselves, but also when we seek to pray for others. Perhaps you've searched for the right words to pray for someone in their moment of need and struggled to find them. Or you've longed to ask God to intervene in your life, but you can't seem to turn your longings into sentences. I know I've often settled for less than what my heart ached to pray for, not for lack of thought or care, but simply an inability to articulate myself in the way I desired to.

While we've seen in the previous chapter that there are times for silent prayer, there are also countless circumstances when prayer requires words. Many situations demand that we bring our petitions and requests to God (Phil 4:6). In hard times, where can we go to find the right words to pray? What language do we use when we experience hardship, or look on at the suffering of someone else and want to intercede on their behalf? How can we offer comfort, hope and peace to others when life feels hopeless, and words seem distant?

In this chapter I want to introduce us to a practice as old as the church itself: the practice of praying the Scriptures (Acts 4:24–26). This practice is one that leads us directly to the deepest well of words that we could ever draw from—God's own words. We're going to see together that the Scriptures are the source that we can turn to and find language for our longings and suffering. In our inability to articulate our empathy for the pain of others and when we're unsure of what to even pray for, the Scriptures offer us words to take up as our own and offer on behalf of others. It may sound strange, perhaps even ungenuine, to take the words of Scripture and pray them as if they're our words, but my hope throughout this chapter is that together we'll see the beauty, richness, and peace that is extended through learning to pray the Scriptures.

Praying the Scriptures

About two years after my sister, Rach, had died, I remember a shift taking place in my prayer life. I moved from a season that had been characterized by the overwhelming sadness, confusion, and anger that came with the early stages of grief, into a place where my pain was less sharp, and stability and trust in God was slowly increasing in my life. As this change began to take place, I noticed that the prayers I was praying started to change too. My prayers moved from raw, emotion-filled lament to a form that was clutching for greater substance and depth of expression. The only problem was I didn't know how to pray like that. This was particularly true when I prayed for other people experiencing hurt; I wanted to somehow show that I understood their pain with the prayers I prayed and that I was willing to enter it in some way—yet I kept coming up short of expressing my thoughts and the depth of my concern appropriately.

At that point I ended up having a conversation with a mentor who walked me through how to "pray the Scriptures." Having grown up in church, it was a familiar line. I'd occasionally heard someone say that as Christians "we pray the Scriptures" and nodded my head in agreement as if it made total sense. But in truth, I had no idea what that phrase really meant. Was I supposed to repeat the verses I read back to God verbatim? My life seemed to have unique challenges, so were my prayers restricted to what was mentioned in the Bible? And how was I ever meant to remember what the Bible said when it came time to pray?

It turned out to be far simpler than I envisaged. Here's what it boiled down to: we use the language given to us by God in the Scriptures as the point of reference for the words we offer back to God in prayer. Tim Keller helpfully explains this in terms of a conversation: "Prayer is continuing a conversation that God has started through his Word and his grace."[1] In other words, the conversation has been initiated by God already through the Scriptures and in the story contained within its pages, and prayer is how we respond to what he has said. It's like any other conversation we have with people, where we either reply to the words spoken to us or start a conversation based upon the relationship we have with that person or the shared context that we're in.

What I discovered was that praying the Scriptures really means praying prayers that are directly informed by and a response to what we read in the word of God. It offers a way for us to pray in the hardship and mess of our lives that is clear; God's given us promises, stories, songs, and prayers in the Bible, and we use them as the substance of our prayers in response. When we don't know what we should be praying in any given circumstance, we can open our Bibles and pray in response to what God has said about the situation we find ourselves in.

Sure, we might not always see a direct parallel between our situation and one in the Bible, but as we'll see throughout this chapter, God's word is remarkably wide-reaching in the circumstances it applies to. The Scriptures show us how to pray in all seasons by lamenting in times of grief and sorrow and praising God in the moments of joy. We learn how to be thankful and how to repent, what it means to petition God and how to intercede for others. When we don't know what or how to pray, and words seem far from our minds, the Scriptures are a gift to us, reminding us to pick up the conversation right where God left it. They help us to cut through the uncertainty of not knowing what to pray by offering us peace in the form of words that we can pray in response to God.

I've also found that using the Scriptures as a guide for my prayers provides with me a guardrail for when my priorities and desires would otherwise slide off track. They redirect my wayward heart and mind back towards God's purposes and peace. At times we can all be prone to reacting to our feelings and frustrations in less than helpful ways, but praying the Scriptures is a practice that allows us to embrace a truer reality than what we might presently

1. Keller, *Prayer*, 54.

see or feel. It helps us to find the right focus, direction and shape for our prayers that could otherwise remain elusive.[2] In essence, praying the Scriptures is praying for God's will to be done and not just our own.

If we want to take up this practice for ourselves though, there are two key questions that need to be answered; what parts of Scripture do we turn to if we want to pray? And how do we then incorporate them into our prayers? The next two sections will look to answer each of these questions in turn.

What Parts of Scripture Should I Pray?

There are no hard and fast rules when it comes to choosing a part of Scripture to pray in your time of need or someone else's moment of pain. Providing you've considered the context of a passage and know you're not completely misapplying it; you should feel confident to allow the Scriptures to fuel your prayers. We're told that all of God's word is useful and purposeful in different moments, and it should be the primary source that teaches us to pray (2 Tim 3:16).

However, there are three places in the Scriptures that I want to draw our attention to here: the Psalms, the Lord's Prayer, and passages that declare promises from God. There are other great parts of Scripture to be prayed through, such as the prayers of the apostle Paul, the Sermon on the Mount in Matthew's Gospel, and the Upper Room Discourse in John's Gospel to name only a few. I've chosen the three outlined below because they're particularly relevant and helpful for our purpose of praying in hard times, and my hope is that they'll be a beneficial place to start your practice of praying the Scriptures.

Praying the Psalms

In the practice of lament, we spoke about befriending the Psalms, and my encouragement here is to take that even deeper by actively

---

2. Guthrie, *I'm Praying for You*, 15.

praying the words of the psalmists. Ancient Israel viewed the Psalter as their prayer book to help them approach God in prayer, and the first verses of Scripture that the early church incorporates into their own expression of prayer comes from Psalm 2 (Acts 4:24–26). We'd do well to learn from their example and actively take up the language of the psalms, allowing them to shape and form our prayers to God. Part of the reason for this is the incredible range of circumstances and difficulties that they speak to, as well as the variety of forms that they express.

The late pastor and author Eugene Peterson noticed this throughout his lifetime in ministry: "The Psalms train us to pray with others who have prayed, and are praying: put our knees on the level with other bent knees; lift our hands in concert with other lifted hands; join our voices in lament and praise with other voices who weep and laugh."[3] When you seek words to pray in your own moments of hardship, look to the words of the psalmists and make them your prayer before God too. We stand in a long line of faithful saints who've prayed these same words in moments of need, and they've stood the test of time. If you're unsure of how to pray for someone in their time of hurt or heartache, remember the Psalms are a treasure trove for faithfully expressing your solidarity, empathy, and dependence upon God alongside those you suffer with.

Praying the Lord's Prayer

This might not be the first prayer that comes to mind in times of suffering, but the Lord's Prayer (Matt 6:9–13 and Luke 11:2–4) is a prayer that touches every circumstance we face. It keeps us from becoming too introspective when hardship is close at hand by teaching us to pray in accordance with God's will, priorities, and desires in all seasons of life. The Lord's Prayer does this by lifting our eyes to our need for forgiveness, demonstrating dependence upon God for the provision of our daily bread, and praising our Father for who he is. It also prevents us from forgetting about those

---

3. Peterson, *Answering God*, 19.

who suffer by asking for God's kingdom to come—the kingdom that reverses the curse of sin, suffering, and death in our world—and brings hope through Jesus. When we pray the Lord's Prayer, it holds all of the realities of life together and brings them before God, acknowledging that he cares for people in all circumstances.

Martin Luther, the great reformer of the sixteenth century, had a particularly helpful practice for praying the Lord's Prayer. He encouraged believers to pray this prayer every day and to personalize each section of it according to the needs and desires that arose that day: "I do not bind myself to such words or syllables, but say my prayers in one fashion today, in another tomorrow."[4] I've found Luther's practice helpful in my own life, primarily because it takes the priorities of this prayer that Jesus taught, and uses it as a model that provides a place for every circumstance of every day to be brought before God in prayer. It intertwines God's priorities with the realities of our lives instead of praying the words verbatim. In doing so, it guides the process of praying and keeps us on track. When you're searching for the words to pray in moments of trial, returning to the Lord's prayer will tune your heart to the desires of God and, in time, also nourish your prayers for your greatest needs and the requests of others.

Praying the Promises of God

We're told in the Scriptures that we have a God who is a promise-maker and promise-keeper (Ps 145:13). That means when we pray to our Father in heaven and ask him to be faithful to the promises he has made in Scripture, we can have confidence that he will remain true to his word. We can pray God's promises from countless passages in Scripture, but one example is the promise we're given in both Deuteronomy 31:6 and Hebrews 13:5 that God will never leave or forsake those that belong to him. This was true for the people of Israel in the Old Testament, as well as those that believe

---

4. Parrish, "Simple Way to Pray," 35.

Finding Peace through Prayer

in Christ in the New Testament. Below are some examples of how we could pray this promise from God in different situations:

> "Thank you, Father, that you will never leave me or forsake me in my time of need."

> "Lord, I don't feel your presence right now, but I believe your promise to never leave me or forsake me. Please keep your promise to me and be with me in my struggles today."

> "God, I pray for (include person or circumstance in time of need), please continue to be with them and remind them that you will never leave them or forsake them despite their hardships."

This is a promise that transcends time, place, and culture, making it profoundly comforting, reassuring, and necessary to cling to in hard times. One of the beautiful realities about many of God's promises is that we can pray a particular promise, such as the one above, in countless unique circumstances and it will remain relevant and true. We can also confidently declare these promises in our prayers and remain insistent upon God's faithfulness in response because we know that God's character, as revealed to us in Jesus, remains the same yesterday, today, and forever (Heb 13:8). Beginning to pray the promises of God grounds us in eternal truths when the earth is shaking beneath our feet. It clarifies our requests and petitions by reminding us of what God has promised to do for us. And it provides us with words of assurance in the uncertainty of life's circumstances.

Praying God's promises has been a lifeline for me, and I pray they will be for you too. Before we look at some practical ways to incorporate the Scriptures into our prayers, I want to give you an example of how I've prayed the Scriptures in a moment of personal and collective need. A few years ago, I sat with my Aunty Robyn in my parents living room, knowing that her battle with pancreatic cancer was likely to be terminal. Nothing though could have

60

prepared me for the gut-wrenching question she'd ask that day: "Mitch, will you take my funeral service?"

I wanted to say "no" because I wanted her to remain with us. I wanted my prayers for her cancer to disappear to be answered. Instead, I told her that if the time came, I would take the service. Several months later, that time did come.

It was the first funeral service I'd ever taken, and I ached over what to say. How do you find the words to speak when you're grieving, let alone when you need to speak to others in their grief? I had no idea, until I turned to the Scriptures. To conclude the service, I read from Psalm 121 and prayed a prayer in response as way of offering comfort in a time of mourning. These are the words from that day, with the exclusion of some family names and details:

> In Psalm 121 we read these words of comfort and assurance in our time of grief and sadness:
>
> 1 I lift up my eyes to the mountains—
>   where does my help come from?
> 2 My help comes from the Lord,
>   the Maker of heaven and earth.
> 3 He will not let your foot slip—
>   he who watches over you will not slumber;
> 4 indeed, he who watches over Israel
>   will neither slumber nor sleep.
> 5 The Lord watches over you—
>   the Lord is your shade at your right hand;
> 6 the sun will not harm you by day,
>   nor the moon by night.
> 7 The Lord will keep you from all harm—
>   he will watch over your life;
> 8 the Lord will watch over your coming and going
>   both now and forevermore.
>
> Heavenly Father,
> Thank you that our help comes from you, the Maker of heaven and earth. We need your help right now Lord as we grieve. Please comfort each of us here today and in the days ahead in our grief, and we ask that you would be true to your word by watching over each of us,

particularly Robyn's family. When days feel dark and difficult, and we question why this has happened, help us to lift our eyes to look at you, and be the shade at our right hand by giving us peace, care, and assurance of your love. Please continue to watch over our comings and goings, watch over our lives Lord, as you watched over Robyn's. Give us courage to learn from and give you thanks for Robyn's life. Thank you, Father, for the reality of the hope we have in the life to come—and that you watch over us eternally. We thank you for every moment we were able to spend with Robyn, and we long for the day when we see her again in your presence, Lord. Thank you for the gift of Robyn's life, in the name of Jesus we entrust her to you, both now and forevermore. Amen.

How to Pray the Scriptures

The final part of this practice to consider is how to incorporate the Scriptures into our prayers. Sometimes verses from the Bible will infiltrate our prayers just by reading them and resonating with the language. But more often than not, Scripture informs the language of our prayers through intentional choices. Here are four practical steps to help you intentionally implement this practice in your own prayer life:

Record Verses of Scripture

Shortly after the conversation with my mentor about the value of praying the Scriptures, I began to start keeping note of verses that could fuel my prayers. Before long I had hundreds of verses written down. I quickly realized that my prayer life was deeper, richer, and wider because I wasn't trying to remember what was worth praying for each time I came before God, but rather I had a deep well of God's own words to draw upon, respond to, and take up as my own. Perhaps this is my nerdy side coming out, but over time I even began to arrange them in a note in my phone according to certain circumstances in my life that they spoke to—moments of thankfulness, times of despair, a day of disappointment, weeks of tiredness, seasons of doubt and so on. By recording verses of Scripture as I read them, I found solace on days when I knew I needed to talk to God with words but didn't have the right ones to offer. This is a simple step you could take as you read your Bible each day, by recording a single verse that stands out to you in a notepad, journal, or on your phone. By getting in the habit of regularly doing this, it will help to make praying the Scriptures a natural part of your time with God as well—not only when words are hard to come by.

Share a Prayer When You Share a Verse

Over the years, I've received countless messages with Bible verses to encourage me in times of hardship. I appreciate every single one of those messages, and I believe God's word holds incredible power to transform us every time we read it. The reality is though, sometimes we share a verse of Scripture in a message or as an encouragement to someone in their moment of need and feel as though we've extended all the comfort and compassion that we possibly can. Perhaps we subtly think, "It's God's word, what else could we offer?" Truthfully, the verses we've shared can often become white noise among the suffering that person is experiencing. At times it can even be perceived as less thoughtful than using your own words when it's given with little to no explanation or context.

The greatest sources of strength and comfort that I've received have been the handful of times that people have shared verses of Scripture with me, and then written a prayer in response to the verses or told me specifically what they were praying for in view of the verses they'd shared. Why has that been a greater comfort? Because they not only shared the words of God with me, but also took the time to intercede on my behalf in response to those words from God. I remember one time that someone sent me a prayer they prayed in response to Rom 5:1–5, asking that God would grow character, perseverance, and hope in my life despite my suffering. It had such a significant effect on me that I even began to pray this same prayer for myself for months afterwards. I hadn't been sure how to pray, but they gave me language for my longings.

Just imagine how uplifting it would be to have someone share a verse of Scripture that they thought you needed to hear—and then proceed to pray those same verses on your behalf to the God who hears and responds to his people. Those kinds of prayers are some of the greatest that you can offer to someone in their time of need, and often they're right in front of us in our Bibles. Whenever you next sit down with someone in a time of hardship, or send them a message on a difficult day; share a verse from the Scriptures—but also take a moment to pray that verse for them. I can almost guarantee it will lift their soul like little else can.

Write Your Prayers

It has been a practice of mine for several years now to write out prayers based on verses of Scripture when I'm finding words are hard to come by. Perhaps I'm drawn to this practice because of my upbringing in an Anglican church, where liturgy was woven into the fabric of my faith. But I think it's also because I know of no other way to express the depths of despair inside me when suffering feels thick, and hope feels thin.

To me, the beauty of written prayer is the opportunity it affords to linger with the words we choose to offer before God. It gives me time to dwell with the Scriptures and allows them to give language and form to the prayers that I otherwise couldn't and wouldn't pray. Sure, there is a time for raw and unfiltered cries, as well as spontaneous requests and petitions. However, I find that carefully penning my prayers is a way of heeding the wisdom of the teacher in Ecclesiastes: "Guard your steps when you go to the house of the Lord" (Eccl 5:1). It helps me to consider my own heart and align it with God's before I come to him. But is also helps me in tangible ways to pray for others, like the prayer I wrote and prayed at my aunt's funeral. It's not something I do every day, or every week even. I find myself returning to this practice more often in times of national or global tragedy, and when choosing my own words to pray might feel underwhelming or ill-informed in view of the situation someone is experiencing. It can take time to feel comfortable writing your prayers, so my encouragement is to begin with just a line or two of Scripture and consider how you could use the language found there to shape a prayer back to God.

Praying the Prayers of Other Believers

Since the beginning of the church, many faithful saints have written and recorded prayers that sprung from their reading of Scripture, and they've proved to be helpful for many other believers along the way. At times, reading the Scriptures and turning them into a prayer might feel beyond our reach, and this is where taking up the written prayers of saints throughout church history can be a source of strength and grace to us. Tish Harrison Warren describes how praying the prayers of other believers can come to our aid in times of need: "When we are weary, it can help to throw ourselves onto what has come before us, the steady practices of prayer that the church has handed down for safe keeping, for this very moment when we come to the end of ourselves."[5]

In truth, this single point could fill an entire chapter on its own. Praying the prayers of other believers has been a crutch I've leaned on when I've felt weak and without words. Instead of devoting a lot of space to explaining the value of praying the prayers of others, I wanted to mention three books that contain dozens of prayers from throughout the church's history. My hope is that these prayer books might be a blessing to you as you use them, but also a great example of how other believers have prayed prayers based upon the Scriptures.

The first book that has been a blessing to me is the Book of Common Prayer, complied by Thomas Cranmer, the archbishop of Canterbury during the sixteenth century. It contains passages of Scripture to read as well as prayers that stand alongside them, prayers to mark the morning and evening, and psalms, creeds, and

5. Harrison Warren, *Prayer in the Night*, 110.

thanksgivings. The second is *The Valley of Vision*, a compilation of prayers from centuries of Puritan pastors. The Puritans were known for their devotion to prayer and to the Scriptures, and the prayers in *The Valley of Vision* beautifully capture this dedication. A more recent work is *Every Moment Holy*, by Douglas McKelvey, which has modern liturgies for a variety of seasons, struggles, and situations. His follow up book, *Every Moment Holy, Vol 2: Death, Grief, and Hope*, is particularly relevant to praying in hard times and has given me language to express myself on difficult anniversaries, birthdays, and times of continued grieving. Each of these books provides language to help us to express faith, love, and hope in God when words might be hard to find, and I trust they'll enrich your trust in Jesus if you use them—just as they've done for me.

In John's Gospel we read that Jesus is the Word who became flesh and made his dwelling among us (John 1:14). John tells us that Jesus is the light that shines in the darkness and that the darkness has not overcome him (John 1:5). When we pray the Scriptures, we're using the words given to us by the Word to push back the darkness in this world and in our lives. We lean into a reality beyond the one we presently experience and ask the light of the world to shine into the cracks and crevasses that need him most. Taking up the words of the author of life is where we ought to turn when we struggle to find words to express our longings and heartache. When you look on at the hurt and hardships that others experience, use the language graciously given to you by Jesus, the light of life. We know from the Scriptures that the peace of Christ will guard our hearts and minds when we pray, and there is no better place to begin than by praying the Scriptures themselves (Phil 4:7). As you turn to the Scriptures and pray them,

> May the God of hope fill you with all joy and peace as you trust in him, so that you may overflow with hope by the power of the Holy Spirit. (Rom 15:13)

Compassionate Release

For those whose hearts are overwhelmed

"Compassion" is a word that is often used without much thought given to its true meaning. It has Latin origins and is a combination of a prefix *com* and a root word *pati*. *Pati* means "to suffer," and it's where we get words like "passion" from, as well as phrases such as the passion of the Christ. The prefix *com* means "with," and English words like *compatible* and *companion* originate from the same prefix. Together, *com* and *pati* form the word "compassion," meaning "to suffer with."[1]

I'm not sure about you, but when I consider showing compassion toward someone, it doesn't immediately bring to mind suffering with them. I think of something a little closer to showing empathy and being willing to listen or act on someone's behalf. But in the New Testament when both Peter and Paul call followers of Jesus to "be compassionate" (1 Pet 3:8) and to "be kind and compassionate to one another" (Eph 4:32), they're issuing a

---

1. "Understanding the Meaning of Compassion," sec 3.

non-negotiable mandate to Christians that they suffer with those who are suffering. Both apostles are calling believers to model their lives on Christ, the one who displayed the ultimate example of compassion by entering humanity and suffering with and for each of us.

In many ways, this ethic has been central to the work and witness of the church since the beginning. The early church was known for embodying compassion by entering places of hardship and hurt in our world, particularly the lives of their neighbors who were heartbroken or experiencing crippling health issues. This would be a profoundly difficult task in any time and society, but I can only imagine how disorienting it was for the first Christians to be called to live in such a way. By choosing to suffer with those in their local communities, it meant grieving with those who were grieving the loss of family and friends to sickness, famine, and plague. It included caring for those who experienced poverty as well as those neglected by oppressive societies. And it involved praying for and being present with those who were unwell for all manner of reasons. It truly would have been a monumental challenge in their context.

And yet I can't help but feel we live in a time with our own unique challenges when it comes to showing compassion, "suffering with" those who suffer. Our challenge may not always come with the same proximity to the depths of intense suffering that the early church faced. Instead, we are faced by an incomparable breadth of hardship. In the digital age we have access to and knowledge of the entirety of the world's suffering at our fingertips. And it's beginning to overwhelm our ability to show compassion and our capacity to pray in response.

Allow me to explain a little further. If your phone is nearby, pick it up for a moment. Turn it over in your hands. Notice how compact and light it is. Feel the ease with which it rests in your palm, almost as though it's an extension of yourself. Right now, you hold the ability to access an endless amount of information. More news about the world is accessible at the touch of your screen than there has been for any other generation of people who have *ever* lived. We live in a world where the amount of news, notifications, and information that floods our screens is simply too vast for us to process, let alone empathize with. Most millennials and members of Gen Z, the generations born after 1981, spend close to five hours per day on their phones.[2] Research shows that six to seven times every hour we reach into our pockets, take out our glowing screens, and check what is happening in the world beyond what we see in front of our eyes.[3] Why do I bring all this to your attention? It's not to make you feel guilty, but because we've become overloaded with information, and it's causing us to be overwhelmed as we process it.

Just this week I read an article in the *New York Times* titled "There Are Almost Too Many Things to Worry About."[4] And it's almost true. I say "almost" true because there aren't "almost" too many things to worry about—there *are* too many things to worry about. The entire weight of the world's collective hardship, suffering, pain, and death is now accessible to each of us at every moment of the day. For better or worse, and whether we like it or not, every problem known to humanity is being channeled into our lives via our devices. The result is that we're not only aware of what is happening in our own corner of the world and our local communities, but we've become acutely aware of the circumstances unfolding all over the globe in real time. And sadly, much of what we see, hear, and know about revolves around suffering. It means there are not only too many things to "worry about," but also too many people and problems for us to pray compassionately on behalf of. It can simply feel overwhelming and peace-sapping for those of us who long to intercede, let alone for those of us are already weighed down with anxiety and worry in our own lives.

When faced with such a breadth of human hardship, what are we to do? How can we possibly show compassion for people near and far without being overwhelmed? And how are we to pray

---

2. Paul, "Millennials Waste Five Hours A Day," para. 2.
3. Naftulin, "Here's How Many Times We Touch Our Phones," para. 2.
4. Collins and Stephens, "Almost Too Many Things," para. 1.

in a world with a never-ceasing news cycle that informs us of the hardships of all humanity?

The practice of *Compassionate Release* provides a way of praying in precisely this predicament. Compassionate release is a practice that helps us to see prayer as an act of "suffering with" others, while also acknowledging we cannot hold all the suffering in our world. Instead, we're invited to release our fears and worries to the God who can hold the hardships of all humanity. Compassionate release is a form of prayer that acknowledges our limited capacity to suffer with and pray for every hardship we see, while still committing the needs of the world to our God who is limitless in his compassion for humanity. Before we learn to take up this prayer practice ourselves, let's consider how prayer can be an act of compassion—and why it feels so hard to do.

Prayer Is Compassionate, but We Have Compassion Fatigue

Prayer is often the most powerful way we can show compassion toward those we are not physically present with. There are certainly other ways of showing compassion: raising money for particular causes, phone calls to loved ones in other places who are experiencing hardship, or increasing awareness of the plight of people who are marginalized or disadvantaged. We should and must engage in compassion in ways such as these. But prayer is a unique demonstration of compassion because it's a way of bringing the petitions and requests of those in need before "the Father of compassion and the God of all comfort, who comforts us in all our troubles" (2 Cor 1:3–4). It shows compassion because it brings the suffering of the afflicted before the One who is the source and origin of all compassion. The writings of the apostle Paul are saturated with this truth:

> Yes, and I will continue to rejoice, for I know that through your prayers and God's provision of the Spirit of Jesus Christ what has happened to me will turn out for my deliverance. (Phil 1:18–19)

He has delivered us from such a deadly peril, and he will deliver us again. On him we have set our hope that he will continue to deliver us, as you help us by your prayers. (2 Cor 1:10–11)

And pray in the Spirit on all occasions with all kinds of prayers and requests. With this in mind, be alert and always keep on praying for all the Lord's people. Pray also for me, that whenever I speak, words may be given me so that I will fearlessly make known the mystery of the gospel, for which I am an ambassador in chains. (Eph 6:18–20)

In each of these verses, Paul has or is being faced with a moment of trial or difficulty. How does he say the church at Corinth and Philippi helped him in his time of need? By praying for him. What does he ask for from the church at Ephesus, even while in chains? It's not entering his jail cell with him, but engaging in prayer for him. This is how they suffer with Paul, and he believes it makes a difference. Paul also attributes being delivered from deadly peril to prayer, and has hope that through prayer it will happen again—even if only in an eternal capacity (2 Cor 1:10–11). He can rejoice in his difficulties because he knows God will bring about deliverance in the midst of his hardships (Phil 1:18–19). And he urges the Ephesians to "keep on praying for all the Lord's people," bringing all their requests to God, because there's an unwavering trust in God's faithfulness to answer prayer (Eph 6:18–20). Prayer is compassionate according to Paul. It's how we enter into suffering from a distance. It also possesses the power to comfort people and alter circumstances. As theologian Pierce Taylor Hibbs says, "taking the time to pray is one of the simplest and most powerful ways you can give yourself to others."[5] Prayer is a simple yet potent act of self-giving and compassion because it brings the burdens of another person before their great Deliverer and Comforter; the One who can empathize completely with their weakness as well as change their circumstances according to his will.

5. Hibbs, *Finding Hope in Hard Things*, 56.

And yet while it's a wonderful privilege to know prayer is a means of showing compassion, it is also where the difficulty being addressed in this chapter arises. We long to pray in the way Paul is describing here, but the reality is that many of us feel overwhelmed by the number of situations to show compassion toward—and it can become paralyzing. This feeling has become so pervasive that psychologists have coined a new term to describe it: "compassion fatigue." Compassion fatigue is defined as "the cost of caring for others or for their emotional pain, resulting from the desire to help relieve the suffering of others."[6] It sounds eerily like the struggle we've been naming. Professor and theologian Kelly Kapic suggests that it "describes the reaction of our limited capacity and the unlimited need."[7] We can't keep up. We are limited, and the reality of our age is we're readily aware of the unlimited need that exists. We rightly feel fatigued and strained when attempting to bring all of it before God in prayer. It's wearing us down and exhausting us of any kind of peace that is possible to possess in Christ. All too often as I speak to faithful Christians, I hear that they end up feeling overwhelmed to the point of prayerlessness because understandably, they cannot cope with the scope of suffering they're seeing and hearing about. This is an increasingly difficult position that many of us find ourselves in—and it's not going away.

Let me give you an example. As I pen these words, the world feels like it's in a downward spiral. Ukraine has just been invaded by Russia in a swift and destructive war that no one saw coming. There are families being torn apart, a country being bombed, and countless people who have lost their lives. Every hour for the first two weeks of the war I received an update on my phone, notifying me of the latest news. I chose to get these updates, because I wanted to be informed as I prayed, lamented, and interceded for the atrocities that were occurring. I couldn't be physically present, but my desire to show compassion drove me to my knees in prayer. While this has been playing out before my eyes, two states in Australia—Queensland and New South Wales—have experienced

6. "Compassion Fatigue"
7. Kapic, You're Only Human, 168.

devastating flooding. These areas have been ravaged to the point where homes have been swept away by the rising floodwaters, taking lives and livelihoods with them. Again, I've been lamenting and asking God to intervene.

There's also been a fresh wave of COVID-19 infections across the globe, continuing a now two-year pandemic that has shut-down the world, killed millions, and affected every single person on the planet. I haven't just seen the effects on my local community; I've seen the effects on every community around the world. It's all part of the groundswell of information that I've inevitably received. Right now, it feels like there has been a barrage of unrelenting and overwhelming events, and it's been impossible to avoid the collective weight of turmoil, tragedy, and grief that has accumulated.

Amidst all this, there's also a myriad of difficulties closer to home that are taking their own toll. In the last week my wife lost her grandmother to COVID, a young woman in our small group received a harrowing medical diagnosis, and a friend was let go from their job. It's often these moments that sting the most; the loss of loved ones or jobs, the death of dreams, and the sight of sick friends. When hardship hits those closest to us, we're reminded that those who occupy our newsfeeds are real people, with real hurt and heartache. It often heightens our desire to show compassion, while providing a reality check about the scale of suffering that is present around the globe. I'm sure you feel this too. No matter where or when you're reading these words, there's an incalculable amount of pain that is present in our world in the form of wars, famine, illness, inequality, or natural disasters. I imagine there is undoubtedly a steady stream of suffering infiltrating your life or the lives of those you hold dear. How can we possibly bear up under the weight of that realization, and pray compassionately for everyone and everything being affected?

The glaring problem that arises is we can't hold all this hardship in our hearts and minds without becoming overwhelmed and experiencing compassion fatigue. It's simply too much to bear. We have a natural desire as followers of Jesus to show compassion to those who are suffering, and to pray for those in need—just as the early church does for Paul and others in times of hardship. But when we stare at the sum of the world's sorrows, it's more likely to rob us of our peace and paralyze our prayers than drive us to come before God and intercede for justice, mercy, and comfort for the afflicted.

This is why the practice of compassionate release is so vital for believers today. It's not only our peace in Christ that is impacted when we cease to pray or fail to faithfully navigate these difficulties, but also the peace of those for whom we're called to compassionately pray for.

Compassionate Release

Prayers of compassionate release are intended to serve two important purposes: firstly, to recognize that showing compassion is our desire and it is needed for the circumstance or person enduring suffering, and secondly to release this same suffering to God because we cannot hold it all ourselves on top of the hardships which we are already praying for or experiencing. It acknowledges that we are finite, and God is infinite. It humbly accepts the limits of our own capacity for compassion and depends upon the limitless nature of the Father of compassion.

Perhaps the most helpful way to explain the practice of compassionate release though is with an example. In the prayer of compassionate release that I've included below, I use "circumstance/person" as a catch-all way of representing the situation, injustice, tragedy, person, or group of people that you might be seeking to bring before God compassionately and release to him. You can replace this with the name of the person or the circumstance that you're praying for and elaborate as freely as you would like to. The practice of compassionate release is one of saying:

> Heavenly Father,
> Thank you that you are the God of all comfort and the Father of compassion.
> I look on and see the suffering of (include circumstance/person), and I long to have the compassion for this circumstance/person that you do.

You know my limitations, Lord. You know I lack the capacity to suffer with everyone, but I know you are able
to—for you are limitless.
So, I hand this circumstance/person into your caring
hands, for you alone can carry this burden. I release this
circumstance/person to you Father, and I plead that you
would act in a way that is compassionate, comforting,
merciful, and just.
In Jesus' name,
Amen.

This prayer might feel a little rigid the first time you pray it,
but I promise you it helps me almost daily when I'm confronted
with the depth and breadth of suffering in our world. You'll notice
it does something we've spoken about throughout this book; it
calls upon God to be true to his character in the way that he acts
and responds to our prayers. This lies at the heart of prayers of
compassionate release, and it also allows us to let go of the worries
that are too much for us to hold by releasing them to God.

This is why the apostle Peter commands believers to "cast all
your anxieties on him because he cares for you" (1 Pet 5:7). Peter
is writing in a context where "the family of believers throughout
the world is undergoing the same kind of sufferings," meaning that
both the audience he is writing to and Christians around the world
are experiencing significant hardships (1 Pet 5:7–9). And what's
his command in these circumstances? To cast, or more literally
"throw," their pressures and burdens onto God. It means ceasing
to hold the difficulties you carry by handing them to someone else.
That's not because the believers are told not to care or have any
compassion toward others, but because the One who catches their
worries has an endless capacity for caring and they don't.

The reality is God already knows our fears and our anxieties,
the burdens we carry, and the endless stream of sorrows that we
hear about. They never surprise him. But it's in the act of praying
that we're able to release these concerns to God, remembering that
he cares for us deeply and is pouring out compassion upon those
we pray for. Compassionate release is far from a passive reluctance
to engage in the struggles of life, it's an active choice to cast the

cares of all creation upon our Creator. According to Peter, God *wants* us to do that because he knows it will help us. It's more than a nice suggestion, it's a practice of putting the situations that overwhelm us into the hands of the One who offers peace in return. And importantly, it's possible to do that with compassion, because we know the character of the God to whom we commit them. In his book *Get Your Life Back*, author John Eldredge describes the necessity of this practice:

> You've got to release the world; you've got to release people, crises, trauma, intrigue, all of it. There has to be sometime in your day where you just let it all go. All of the tragedy of the world, the heartbreak, the latest shooting, earthquake—the soul was *never* meant to endure this. The soul was never meant to inhabit a world like this. It's way too much. Your soul is finite. You cannot carry the sorrows of the world. Only God can do that. Only he is infinite. Somewhere, sometime in your day, you've just got to release it. You've got to let it go.[8]

Eldredge touches on one of the core reasons why the practice of compassionate release is necessary: we're finite, and God is infinite. That's why we're invited to cast our fears upon the one who hears us. We need to release the suffering that is beyond our limitations, or we'll become overwhelmed. Maybe you've never heard this before, but you have permission to hand circumstances and people to God, to release the flood of difficulties that wash over you, and to allow there to be some distance between you and every single struggle being faced around the world today. Part of faithfully following Jesus means acknowledging you have limits on your physical, mental, emotional, and spiritual capacity. You are finite, so you can't do it all. I know that's confronting and humbling to hear, but I hope it's refreshing too. It should lead us to a deeper and richer trust in the limitless and infinite goodness, grace, and love of God. He alone is capable of carrying every ounce of brokenness in this world, and that is part of the good news of the gospel (Matt 11:28–30).

8. Eldredge, *Get Your Life Back*, 24.

Sometimes when I talk to fellow Christians about praying prayers of compassionate release, I get responses like "Aren't we meant to bear one another's burdens?" (Gal 6:2), "Isn't this neglecting the call to practically love our neighbors and seek justice?," or the latest one I heard: "This sounds like self-help clothed in the language of prayer."

These are all valid and helpful questions. The practice of compassionate release could lead to neglecting our responsibility to bear the burdens of those in our lives, and offering a prayer when carrying our share of the struggle is required instead. It could also mean we betray our call to sacrificially love our neighbors or practice justice, mercy, and compassion on behalf of those who need it most, washing our hands of a God-given responsibility. And perhaps it could even descend to a desire to help ourselves feel better by alleviating any sense of "suffering with" those who suffer.

But at its best, the practice of compassionate release actually allows us to engage in our world in a way that is more loving and compassionate. We're called to bear each other's burdens, not everyone's burdens. This practice helps us to take up responsibility for burden-bearing in our families, local churches, and our neighbors without loading ourselves up with the weight of the entire world's worries. It also frees us to engage wholeheartedly and sacrificially in the work of justice, mercy, and compassion that God has led us to, be it locally or globally, while still acknowledging there are other causes worth committing to God in prayer. Otherwise, we may end up ignoring them because we're overwhelmed. And on the question of self-help, praying prayers of compassionate release is primarily a way of helping others and showing compassion toward them by entrusting people and circumstances we otherwise couldn't help in any meaningful way into the hands of the Father of compassion.

If we're honest with ourselves, we know that our capacity isn't big enough to cope with the sum of the suffering placed before our eyes. It's natural, even right, for us to feel out of our depth swimming in the ocean of turmoil we find around us. When we pray prayers of compassionate release, we're choosing to resist our desire to "be like God" and live into our limits instead of denying them (Gen 3:5). Those limits must include practical, embodied work in the lives of those we're called to bear burdens for, advocate on behalf of, or sacrificially give towards. But God knows we can't do it all. Our problem is that we don't often recognize that ourselves. Compassionate release is a form of prayer that acknowledges we are creatures and not the Creator and that we long to see God bring healing, justice, and hope to all.

If you're overwhelmed by the never-ending firehose of bad news being pointed in your direction, then take up the practice of compassionate release. It won't stop you from being saturated with suffering, but it will provide a way to pray that gives yourself compassionately to others by asking God to intervene. Releasing those circumstances or people into the care of God is, in the end, a way of being able to love and show compassion toward those God has given you responsibility for or leads you to suffer with more closely. Begin to cast your fears upon the God who hears you. Learn to accept your limits and finiteness as a gift from God, knowing you can't save—or even carry—the world. And rejoice in knowing that even your short prayers of compassionate release are heard by the infinite God of comfort and the limitless Father of compassion, who is faithful to respond and bear every burden.

Practicing Compassionate Release

I receive an alert on my phone: "Global hunger predicted to rise." It's been a difficult week—I've attended a funeral for a neighbor, spoken with a loved one about their recent diagnosis with depression, and begun to launch a new ministry in our city for refugees and those who are vulnerable. I feel like I've hit my limit, so I open a note in my phone titled "Compassionate Release" and begin to pray the prayer I included earlier before I open the article.

Later that day, I take out my phone and begin to scroll through social media. Inevitably, I learn of a natural disaster, notice someone in need of prayer, and feel my heart sink at the state of our world. I return to my prayer.

That evening, I walk past someone in the city asking for money—they're genuinely in need of practical compassion—true and embodied "suffering with." Stopping for a moment, I ask God to give me the wisdom to know if I should go further in meeting this person's need: "Lord, grant me the wisdom to know whether to enter into this suffering through personal action or deeper prayer." Some days I stop and offer to buy a meal for people in this situation, sitting to have a conversation and hear their story. But today, I open the note in my phone again and pray a prayer of compassionate release—placing this individual into the caring hands of their Creator.

I don't want to ever be closed off from engaging compassionately with those that God places in front of me, but I know I also need to honor my God-given limits. It's a hard line to walk. It requires wisdom. And I have no doubt that I get it wrong at times. We need to know our capacity while allowing God to search our hearts and keep us from selfishness. But practicing compassionate release also means we should pray for a greater capacity for suffering with others, at the same time as being acutely aware of the responsibilities and needs that only we can tend to: our family, friends, local church community, and neighborhood. We all feel this tension, and it's a healthy one for each of us as followers of Jesus to wrestle with. Each of our callings, situations, and limits are unique; only you can truly discern where to put the boundary markers. I do, however, want to offer three practical principles to help with implementing this practice into your life.

1. Have a compassionate prayer to pray

At times, we can default into prayerlessness when we become overwhelmed with the flood of bad news we receive. By having a prayer of compassionate release that is easily accessible, it removes an obstacle to praying. I keep a note in my phone titled "Compassionate Release," but you could have a prayer inside your Bible, beside your bed, or even a short sentence or two memorized that you can draw on as you need. This compassionate prayer could be one you write yourself, the example I gave previously, or the excerpt from the Book of Common Prayer recorded below in the third point. The important part is having a prayer on hand to pray when circumstances arise that you need to commit to God. You might like to decide on a prayer today, to write it somewhere that is useful for you, and then to practice compassionately releasing the circumstance or person you're praying for into the hands of God.

2. Know what makes you overwhelmed

This chapter is written "for those whose hearts are overwhelmed." It's been written with a variety of situations in mind, because for each of us we'll feel burdened by different circumstances and at different times in our lives. The most helpful way of using this practice is to identify what makes you overwhelmed and then begin to pray prayers of compassionate release as you find yourself entering those moments. It could be when you open social media or watch the news and feel the weight of the world's struggles land upon your shoulders; in that case, pray a prayer of compassionate release prior to entering times of consuming media or immediately when you finish that time. Perhaps it's a practice you use to start your day when you know it will be full of people, problems, and painful situations. It may even be beneficial to build into part of your personal quiet times if you find it hard to concentrate on spending time with God amidst the swirling thoughts and concerns that are present in the outside world. By knowing what overwhelms us, we're able to release those burdens to God and leave them in his compassionate arms.

3. Conclude the day with compassionate release

A beautiful summary of all we've learnt in this chapter comes from the Book of Common Prayer, which contains prayer "offices" that mark different intervals throughout the day. At the end of each day, the office of "Compline" is prayed, which simply means "completion."[9] A portion of this prayer office is one of the earliest

9. Eland, *Layman's Guide*, 17.

examples of a prayer of compassionate release, often attributed to Saint Augustine.[10] It reads:

> Keep watch, dear Lord, with those who work, or watch, or weep this night, and give your angels charge over those who sleep. Tend the sick, Lord Christ; give rest to the weary, bless the dying, soothe the suffering, pity the afflicted, shield the joyous; and all for your love's sake. Amen.[11]

Every night for centuries, Christians have prayed these words to release the suffering and difficulties of this world into the hands of their Lord who never slumbers or sleeps, but continues to watch over all people with boundless compassion. It's been a practice that has allowed believers to say with King David, "in peace I will lie down and sleep, for you alone, O Lord, make me dwell in safety" (Ps 4:8), instead of continuing to toss and turn with the endless anxieties of life. We may find it difficult to truly give these situations over to God, but we stand in a long line of faithful followers of Christ who've recognized their limits and clung to the limitlessness of the Father of all compassion. To lie down in peace, we need to entrust the world's problems to the Maker of the world and refuse to hold them all to ourselves.

I pray the practice of compassionate release will allow you to know the peace of Christ in a tumultuous and overwhelming world. To that end, here are the final lines of the office of Compline, and our benediction to conclude this practice:

> Guide us waking, O Lord, and guard us sleeping;
> that awake we may watch with Christ,
> and asleep we may rest in peace.
> The almighty and merciful Lord, Father, Son, and Holy Spirit,
> bless us and keep us.
> Amen.[12]

---

10. Hatchett, *Commentary on the American Prayer Book*, 147. While many people attribute Compline to Saint Augustine, the exact origins are unknown.

11. "An Order of Night Prayer"

12. "An Order for Compline"

In All Circumstances, Give Thanks

For each of us, in every situation

IN 1871, A SUCCESSFUL lawyer and investor by the name of Horatio Spafford lost much of his wealth to the Great Chicago Fire. This was quickly followed by the death of his four-year-old son to scarlet fever, leaving Horatio and his family understandably stricken with grief.

A little while later, Horatio decided that his family needed a vacation, so he sent his wife and four daughters to England by boat, where he intended to join them once he had completed some important work. While the boat was partway across the Atlantic Ocean, it collided with another large ship, sinking within hours. Tragically, all four of Horatio's daughters died in the accident. His wife, Anna, miraculously survived and managed to make it to England. When she arrived, she sent a telegram to Horatio that read, "Saved alone. What shall I do?"

Immediately, Horatio set sail for England. When his ship was midway across the Atlantic, the captain called Horatio to the deck to speak with him. The ship's captain informed him that this was the spot where Horatio's daughters had lost their lives. As he sailed over a place that held much grief and despair, Horatio was also filled with a sense of comfort and peace.[1] He captured this moment by penning these well-known words:

> When peace, like a river, attendeth my way,
> When sorrows like sea billows roll—
> Whatever my lot, thou hast taught me to know
> It is well, it is well with my soul.[2]

Whether you know the much-loved hymn "It Is Well With My Soul" or not, I'm sure you agree: these words are beautifully crafted and testify to a man with a deep faith and trust in God. They capture the depths of suffering that batter us like the waves of the sea, while also recognizing the gentle peace that enters our lives like a river flowing with the grace of God.

What I find most captivating about this hymn, though, are the final two lines of this stanza. How can Spafford truly say that "whatever" his lot in life, whatever comes his way, it is well with his soul? When he was asked a similar question to this, Horatio acknowledged the depths of his pain after losing all five of his children. But he also continued by saying: "In the meantime, thanks to God, we have an opportunity to serve and praise Him for his love and mercy to us and ours. I will praise Him while I have my being."[3]

In the darkest moment of his life, Horatio Spafford was able to give thanks to God. How is this even possible? It's a question I've asked myself many times. And it's the one I want us to consider together now. I'll be honest from the outset—this has been the most difficult chapter of this book to write. It's already a big request to invite you to pray more, not less, during times of suffering. But asking you to develop a practice of giving thanks in the middle of hardship? It feels like I'm stretching the friendship. I've wondered many times if I should skip this chapter completely or change it to something more digestible.

---

1. Petersen, *Be Still My Soul*, 153.
2. "'It Is Well With My Soul'—Spafford Hymn."
3. "'It Is Well With My Soul'—Spafford Hymn."

Over the coming pages we'll see why this practice is necessary, beginning with considering why God asks us to give thanks in all circumstances. After all, it's not just Horatio Spafford who did this—he took his lead from the words of Scripture which encourage us to do the same. We'll then consider how to hold the practice of giving thanks in every situation in tension with practices like lament. They might seem almost contradictory, so we need to learn how to embrace them together. And then finally, we'll learn to look for opportunities to be thankful and consider how to make this a practice that occupies our prayers—even in times of hardship.

Thankfulness *in* All Circumstances, Not Thankfulness *for* All Circumstances

If you cast your minds back to the introduction of this book, you'll remember we looked at Phil 4:6-7. In those verses the apostle Paul explains that through prayer we receive the peace of God in Christ Jesus:

> Do not be anxious about anything, but in every situation, by prayer and petition, with thanksgiving, present your requests to God. And the peace of God, which transcends all understanding, will guard your hearts and your minds in Christ Jesus. (Phil 4:6-7)

I'm not sure if you noticed it the first time, but Paul includes two caveats about how we pray: "in every situation" and "with thanksgiving." When we come before God with our prayers and petitions, we're told to include thanksgiving. And it's not only in certain circumstances, like the joyful and sunny days in life, but in every situation we face. It's easy to gloss over this as peripheral to Paul's main point, or to think that he might be exaggerating. Perhaps that's because it grates against our natural responses to suffering, and on the surface, it seems to clash with practices like lament that validate our cries. But Paul's command is unavoidable: prayer that provides peace is offered with thanksgiving in every situation, not just when we feel like it.

And so that we don't get the wrong picture, Paul isn't sitting at a cozy, safe writing desk at home, penning his ideal morning routine for prayer. He writes from prison, while facing death, and in the middle of persecution (Phil 1:13–14).[4] This isn't a one-off command from Paul either. It's a consistent feature throughout his letters, telling the Ephesians to "always give thanks to God" (Eph 5:20) and the Thessalonians to "give thanks in all circumstances; for this is God's will for you in Christ Jesus" (1 Thess 5:18). Paul is a living, breathing example of what he writes, and he embodies God's will for his life in Jesus.

Despite this constant theme throughout the New Testament, I found this to be a particularly hard practice for me to stomach. Some of the most difficult words I've ever uttered are "I'm thankful for Rach's thirteen years of life." It felt so insincere, wrong even—I wanted a whole life with my sister, not just the beginning of it. I understood the sentiment of being thankful, but I envisaged a future where Rach would graduate high school and live her dreams of helping those less fortunate in whatever capacity she could, where she'd get married and have kids and be a constant source of joy in the lives of those she knew. I wasn't thankful that she was gone—I was heartbroken—so how was I meant to give thanks to God at a time like this? Had Paul missed something in his explanation of prayer?

Once I dug a little deeper into my own struggles with thankfulness, I realized there was truth buried in my confession: I was genuinely thankful to God for Rach's thirteen years of life. It just hurt like hell to not have her with us anymore too. This is a tension we might often feel when we're encouraged to be thankful in times of hardship and suffering; we know we should express our gratitude to God for some things, but we also need meaningful avenues to mourn our losses and grieve the injustices that afflict our lives and the lives of others. In these moments, we can be pulled to one extreme or the other: thankfulness that fails to acknowledge the pain we feel, or lament that neglects to recognize the goodness of God even in seasons of suffering.

4. Crowe, *Grumbler's Guide to Giving Thanks*, 145.

The problem that I had is a common one: I thought I had to be thankful *for* all circumstances, when we're never asked to be. Instead, Paul tells us to be thankful *in* all circumstances. And that single, subtle word change makes all the difference. This is at the heart of Paul's command and also the practice of giving thanks in all circumstances. We offer prayers "with thanksgiving" and "in every situation" because God gives us a reason to be grateful no matter what is happening; he is a good God who offers us the good news that sin, suffering, and death are not the final word because Jesus defeated them through his life, death and resurrection. And that means resurrection glory is our destination no matter how tumultuous the journey is to get there.

What this also means is that we're never, ever asked to give thanks to God for all circumstances—because God is also opposed to the intrusion of suffering in all its forms upon our world. In my case, I'm not asked by God to be thankful that Rach has died, but to express thankfulness for what is worth thanking him for—her joyful life, the gift of a sister, the witness she was to other people, and countless other blessings that came with being her brother. For Horatio Spafford, he wasn't thankful that his children died—as if anyone ever could be—but he saw that there was hope amidst tragedy and he gave thanks to God for it. For you, it doesn't mean you need to be thankful for the suffering and hardship that has entered your life or the life of someone you know; it means that God is asking you to identify how you can continue to give him thanks in those circumstances. It might take time, years even, but the path that God has laid out for us is one that includes thanksgiving along the way.

At this point, the natural question is: how does this practice fit with other practices we've considered so far in this book, specifically the practice of lament?

Holding Thankfulness and Lament Together

Perhaps the idea of holding the practices of lament and thankfulness together feels like a dichotomy, as if I'm trying to have my cake and eat it. But that's the difficult tension that we need to navigate, because the Scriptures refuse to give us the option of choosing between lament and giving thanks, even in times of immense trials.[5]

We find a helpful explanation for how these practices fit together by looking in one of the most unlikely places: the centuries old form of Japanese art called *kintsugi*. The art of *kintsugi* takes broken pottery and pieces it back together. What makes this art form so compelling though, is that the potters don't try to cover up the broken areas by making the pottery look exactly as it did before. Instead, they use a lacquer that is dusted with gold to bind the broken pieces back together in their original place. The final form that this pottery takes not only highlights precisely where it was previously broken—it also makes that brokenness look beautiful, as it's now laced with shining gold. The artists who practice *kintsugi* honor the true history of the pottery rather than simply trying to cover up the blemishes. It's a form of art that dares to make these imperfections not only visible, but the focal point of the pottery, as the gold captures the eye of the observer.

If lament is how we express our pain at the broken pieces of our lives, thankfulness is like the golden lacquer that binds them together by declaring that there remains beauty to be gazed upon in Jesus even when life hurts. Our hardships aren't discarded as uncomfortable or useless fragments of life, they're honored and recognized as part of our journey and are slowly placed back together with care—a care that comes from a God deserving of our gratitude.

Thankfulness is never meant to detract from or gloss over our suffering. It's meant to come alongside it and show that while our heartache is real—so is God and his amazing grace. The practices of lament and thankfulness both point to God's willingness to hear our prayers, respond to them, and be active in our lives. As we lament, we testify that part of God's goodness is his concern for the broken-hearted and his desire to help the afflicted (Ps 147:3). That's precisely why we cry out our complaints and appeal for God to respond when we lament. And then when we practice giving thanks, we take the pieces of our lives that tell stories of

---

5. Kapic, *You're Only Human*, 205.

hurt and hardship, doubt and despair, and place them within the greater story of God redeeming, restoring, and rescuing the world through his son, Jesus. Together, lament and thanksgiving show that our lives are like *kintsugi*: where there are pieces of our journeys that are marked by the brokenness of suffering, yet the whole of our lives are laced with the glorious gold that comes from being found in Christ Jesus.

This means that true and biblical thankfulness is not a doorway out of our pain, but the floor beneath our feet that allows us to keep walking through suffering and hardship. We tread upon the solid ground of God's changelessness amidst our changing circumstances, giving thanks for his dependency and faithfulness despite the situations that we desire to be different.

Over time this has helped me to see that being thankful to God for what we've been given isn't neglecting our pain—it's a way of recognizing why that pain exists in the first place. If Rach's death is worthy of my lament, how much more is her life both here on earth and in eternity worthy of my thankfulness to God? This recognition doesn't strip my pain of its validity; it simply recognizes that there are also reasons to be thankful which are too easily overlooked. This is true of all the moments of suffering in our lives: lament and thankfulness are often two sides of the same coin, where sorrow is sacred, and thankfulness is fitting. Somehow God makes space for both our grumbling and our gratitude, our tears and our thanksgiving. God is not disillusioned by this seeming contradiction, for he knows it's a beautiful picture of the gospel, where death is real but not the final word, because resurrection is certain no matter the circumstances.

While we might be able to now recognize that lament and thankfulness can be held together, we haven't yet considered what we're meant to be thankful for in times of suffering. If Paul isn't encouraging us to be thankful for the specific circumstances we face, what should we be thankful for?

Noticing Opportunities for Thankfulness

In times of hardship, it can be tough to immediately pinpoint anything worthy of thankfulness, and that's understandable. However,
if we're ever going to grow into people who give thanks in every
situation, we need to learn to notice parts of our life that are worth
being thankful for without trivializing our suffering in the process.
While there are countless places that you could look to find reasons to give thanks, I want to suggest three areas of our lives that
each of us can look to in seasons of hardship;

1. Thankfulness for God's Character and Promises

In the Scriptures we're told that the character of God, as revealed in
Jesus, is the same yesterday, today, and tomorrow (Heb 13:8) and
that all of God's promises find their *yes* in Christ (2 Cor 1:20).[6]
This is the starting point for the practice of thankfulness, because
we can always give thanks for these enduring truths about an eternally good and loving God.

   If we want to give thanks for God's character and promises
though, we have to know what God is like and what promises he
has made. To do this, we need to throw ourselves onto the words of
Scripture that declare the beauty of a dependable, strong, and gra-
cious God who never breaks his word. We must plumb the depths
of the gospel story that has at its heart a message about the God
who suffered with and for a rebellious people by sending his son to
die on their behalf. We have to listen with longing and anticipation
to the promises that Jesus' resurrection from the dead will one day
be ours too. And we need to hold onto hope, knowing that when
Jesus returns, every tear will be wiped from our eyes, and every
ounce of suffering will be made right.

   Only then can we respond with thankful prayer. By giving
thanks for God's character and promises, we become tethered to a
reality beyond our present one, a reality that is determined not by
our temporary afflictions but by the confidence we have in God's

---

6. Kapic, *You're Only Human*, 209.

faithfulness, demonstrated undeniably in Jesus. Our situations may be incredibly difficult; there is no denying that. They also may not be resolved or done away with by giving thanks. And yet there is also no doubt about it: we find security, peace, and hope by giving thanks to God for his character and promises—because our lives will always look forward to and long for a greater, eternal home where suffering, sin, and death is defeated in Christ Jesus.

2. Thankfulness to God for His Gifts

The second area that we can find reasons for thankfulness is in the gifts that God gives to us. The book of James declares: "Every good and perfect gift is from above, coming down from the Father of the heavenly lights, who does not change like shifting shadows" (Jas 1:17). This is a timeless truth to cling to: that God is the giver of all gifts and that he will never stop being the source of all that we receive. In response, we ought to give him thanks for those gifts. If we never pause to do so, we miss one half of the story—becoming only lamenters of what has been lost, not thanksgivers for what we've been given.

At times, it is all too easy to receive God's gifts without expressing gratitude and bemoan the loss of those very same gifts further down the track. We can be tempted to pat ourselves on the back when we get a new job, telling ourselves we worked hard and deserved a promotion—only to question what God is doing when we lose that very same job. Likewise, we can take our good health for granted, chalking it up to our good care of our own bodies, until it's stripped away with illness, and we rightly cry out to God. My point is not that we don't deserve promotions or should take no credit at all for anything we have, such as good health. It's simply that we are never the ultimate source of any gift—God is—and therefore, God is worthy of our thanks for every gift we have in life.

If we want to become more aware of God's gifts to us, we need to start by training ourselves to notice God's goodness to us as readily as we notice the lament-worthy moments in life. I appreciate how Kelly Kapic explains this:

Many of us have experienced complex moments that are filled with seemingly inconsistent emotion. We might be thankful for a loved one's peaceful passing, while still experiencing the depth of sorrow and loss. We may be overjoyed that our child got into college, while simultaneously feeling a knot in our stomachs as we cannot imagine how we will pay for it. We can be happy for a friend's promotion at the same moment that we feel the pain of being passed over ourselves. God created in us such an intricate web of emotional response that we can experience complexities so rich that they seem beyond all possibility.[7]

When we give thanks for God's gifts to us in difficult times, it will be hard, complex, and perhaps even feel unnatural or wrong. Yet doing so helps us to live out God's will for our lives as we acknowledge him as the giver of all gifts while embracing the tension of holding hurt and hope alongside one another.

3. Thankfulness for Glimpses of God's Grace

The last area I want to suggest that we search for reasons to be thankful is in glimpses of God's grace in our lives. By glimpses of God's grace, I mean specific moments where we see God working in a way that is kind, loving, generous, merciful, or compassionate in the middle of our present hardships.

In the book of Romans, we're given a powerful and reassuring promise about God's work in all circumstances: "And we know that in all things God works for the good of those who love him, who have been called according to his purpose" (Rom 8:28). I know that verse can be wheeled out in all kinds of occasions, especially when people don't know what to say or aren't sure of how to make sense of a situation. But it's also an incredibly potent promise, filled with the possibility of God actively working even in our suffering. Given that Paul writes this verse in the context of an address about hardships (see practice three, "Embrace Silence"), we can be

7. Kapic, *You're Only Human*, 206–7.

sure it's not a flippant attempt to put on a smile and dismiss our difficulties. Commenting on this verse, Dustin Crowe, author of *The Grumbler's Guide to Giving Thanks*, says, "The Bible doesn't say God might or could use hard things for the good of His people; it says He will do this."[8] We should expect God to be working for good in the middle of hardship and heartache. It might not bring immediate alleviation of our pain, but it will happen—because God has promised it.

We find a great example of this in the life of Charles Spurgeon, a nineteenth century pastor who faced great adversity. He endured long seasons of depression and physical ailments that hampered his health and kept him from his ministry. Pastors, townspeople, and local media despised him—publicly ridiculing his name. He felt anxiety over the weight of preaching and the responsibility of pastoring people.[9] Spurgeon knew what it was like to suffer in a multitude of ways, and yet he fixed his eyes on noticing reasons for gratitude: "Remember the mercies of God. Do not bury them in the grave of ingratitude. Let them glisten in the light of gratitude."[10]

For a long time, I buried the glimpses of God's grace that appeared in my life deep in the soil of ignorance and despair. I neglected to acknowledge before God that prayerful friends were tangible evidence of his grace to me. I refused to admit that a letter of encouragement from an older lady at church was an answer to a prayer I had written in my journal months earlier: "God, if you're there—please encourage me somehow." And I easily glossed over God's kindness to me when I jumped the months-long waiting list to see a psychologist to help me process my grief.

As I look back, I can see that there was a constant thread of God's grace woven into the fabric of the hardest parts of my life, but it's only now that I'm thankful for it. Spurgeon was right; we need to remember God's mercies. We need to notice them and allow them to shine in the light of day, and not overlook the beauty that glimpses of grace hold.

8. Crowe, *Grumbler's Guide to Giving Thanks*, 145.

9. Crowe, *Grumbler's Guide to Giving Thanks*, 151–52.

10. Spurgeon, *Practice of Praise*, 76.

In All Circumstances, Give Thanks

A vital part of the practice of giving thanks in all circumstances is learning to notice opportunities to be thankful. And looking to God's character and promises, his gifts to us, and glimpses of his grace is the perfect place to start. Why not take a few moments now to stop and notice how you can be thankful to God in each of these ways?

Practicing Thankfulness

When Paul tells us to pray with thanksgiving "in every situation," he means we ought to give thanks to God every time we pray (Phil 4:6). That means our practice needs to develop beyond noticing opportunities for giving thanks to God and into a consistent fixture in all our prayers. To make this move from awareness of reasons for gratitude to expression of thanksgiving, I've found three small ways of giving thanks to be helpful: remembering God's past faithfulness at the beginning of my prayers, giving thanks for God's work in the present, and journaling for the future. Together, these smaller steps make up my practice of praying in every situation with thanksgiving and help to fix my eyes on what Jesus has done, is doing, and will do—rather than the temporary circumstances I face. I share them with you not as a rule for how you must give thanks, but as an example that might stir you to implement a similar practice in your own life, where you give thanks to God no matter the situation you find yourself in.

Remember the Past

Whenever I begin my prayers, I've resolved to start by giving thanks to God for his past faithfulness. Normally this flows directly from one of the three areas I mentioned in the previous section. Most often, it's thanking God for his character or promises that I know through the Scriptures, but sometimes it's tied to the generous gifts he's given to me or glimpses of grace I've noticed in the past. By practicing this, it grounds my prayers in a greater reality than the one I'm currently facing, reminding me of who God is despite my circumstances, and that he is faithful and worthy of my thanks.

On a practical level, I've done two things to help me continue giving thanks on days when I would rather do anything else: I record Bible verses that remind me of God's character and promises, and I write them in a note on my phone. As I read through the Bible in my regular quiet times each day, I copy verses that declare God's character and promises into this note. It means that even when God feels distant and I don't feel like giving thanks, I can open my phone and recall them easily rather than flicking through my Bible in search of them. For me, it's become an accessible record of God's past faithfulness as told through the Scriptures. I also keep a journal with glimpses of God's grace that I've noticed and generous gifts that I'm thankful to God for. In times when it's difficult to see how God is working or if I doubt his kindness towards me, I'm able to look in my journal, remember how God has worked in my life in the past, and give thanks for it again.

When we look back and remember God's steadfastness, we find stable ground beneath our feet to continue giving thanks no matter our circumstances. We also locate an enduring source of comfort and hope to pray over the lives of those we minister to. Beginning our prayers by recalling God's prior promises and goodness is a way of steadying our anxious minds and calming our wandering hearts. How could you take a small step toward remembering God's past faithfulness in your prayers?

Give Thanks for the Present

The second small way I've grown my practice of thanksgiving is by naming something specific every day from each of the three areas in the previous section: a character or promise of God, a gift, and a glimpse of grace. My method is to write each of these down in my journal during my quiet times. Then I express thankfulness to God for these things. It means every day the content of my journal grows as I notice who God is or what he's said in his word, a gift in my life that I consciously acknowledge is from the Father of heavenly lights, and an instance of seeing God's mercy, grace, or strength in sustaining me that day. I've found that over time this has anchored me in a place where I express thankfulness to God even when I don't feel thankful, preventing me from being swayed by the feelings of that day. It's taught me to savor what God is doing in my life regularly, and to notice the mundane moments of grace that I would otherwise miss by only looking at the bigger ups and downs.

Perhaps most significantly, this daily routine keeps me attentive to the fact that God didn't only work in the past but remains actively engaged in my life in the present. It's a way of embodying what Paul instructs the church at Colossae to do: "Devote yourselves to prayer, being watchful and thankful" (Col 4:2). Watching for what God is doing helps us continue expressing thanks.[11] We look to God's promises and character in his word, but also his work in the world. While the past activity of God gives us confidence in the present, the more we pay attention to his ongoing work as well, the greater our cause for thanksgiving will be. How can you begin to give thanks to God in the present for his character and promises, his generous gifts, and glimpses of his grace?

Journal for the Future

The last piece of my practice of giving thanks is to record my prayer requests in a journal for the purpose of future thankfulness. I've already mentioned that I can look back on God's faithfulness in the past by looking in my journal, and that's exactly why I continue to journal my prayers and petitions, so that I might have even more reasons to give thanks as time goes by. Perhaps you're not a journaler, and that's okay. You could use a note in your phone or place a piece of paper in the back of your Bible to write prayers down on; the point is simply to make a record of your prayers.

I'm so forgetful that I can't remember what day of the week it is or what I ate for breakfast, let alone what I prayed for last week in a moment of need. If I don't take this step of writing down

---

11. Kapic, *You're Only Human*, 211.

my prayers, I can be prone to praying for a particular struggle for weeks or months, and then barely stop for long enough to give thanks when God answers my prayer. By journaling each day, I ensure that I can rightfully praise God in the future when he answers my prayers in the ways that he sees fit. I'm not always able to recognize the answers, especially when they don't come in the way that I would like, but seeing evidence of God's grace in responding to me over time grows my trust, deepens my faith, and draws me closer to him through the darkest valleys.

As I flick back through my journal, I can see countless answers to prayers that sustain me in hard times: God bringing both of my grandfathers to faith in Jesus just a few weeks before they each passed away, healing a friend of cancer in a miraculous manner that even his doctors couldn't explain, and sustaining my family in practical ways like providing us with a free car through the generosity of a faithful older couple in our church when we had very little money to buy one. There's also plenty of prayers that remain unanswered—but I keep praying knowing that God will continue to hear my prayers. And I also continue giving thanks because I can see a record of his past faithfulness, and it lifts my weary soul to praise God even when I don't feel like doing so. How can you remember the prayers that you pray now, for the purpose of future thankfulness to God?

I asked a slightly pointed question at the beginning of this chapter: how is it possible to say with Horatio Spafford "it is well with my soul" in times of suffering?

Perhaps you still don't feel as though you could say those exact words, and that's okay. My hope though, is that you can see a pathway toward greater gratitude that is not dependent on your circumstances, but on the faithfulness of God. After all, Paul tells the Philippians that as they offer their prayers with thanksgiving in all circumstances, they will receive God's peace in Christ Jesus in return. Their thankfulness precedes their peace. It may be a long road to *feeling* thankful or until the circumstances you face are well with your soul, but the good news is this: we can practice giving thanks to God in every circumstance, no matter how we feel. He is always worthy of our thanksgiving, and that is truly good news.

> May you always have a reason to offer your prayers with thanksgiving,
> knowing that God is faithful and good in every circumstance,
> and may he be true to his promise,
> by providing you with peace in Christ Jesus in return.
> In Jesus' name,
> Amen.

Develop a Rhythm of Prayer

For growing a life of continual prayer

SOME OF THE BEST practical wisdom I've ever heard on prayer is to "keep it simple, keep it real, keep it up."[1] I like the idea of praying in a way that is simple and real—it resonates with me on a deep level. And that's really what the first six practices in this book have focused on: keeping prayer real through honestly coming before God in all circumstances, as well as keeping it simple through practical ways of praying. The part I personally find the hardest, though, is keeping prayer up.

If you're anything like me, sometimes prayer is a struggle. There are days where prayer feels unproductive at best and hopeless at worst. Over the years as I've walked with people through their pain and suffering, I've realized that struggling to pray regularly isn't a difficulty that's unique to me, but something that many people experience when faced with adversity. In fact, many Christians I speak to find it difficult to pray regularly even in the

1. Greig, *How to Pray*, 30.

more mundane seasons of life, let alone when life is hard. This begs the question: how do we keep up a practice of prayer? After all, the New Testament is littered with the encouragement to pray regularly: see Eph 6:18–20, Phil 4:6–7, Col 4:2–4, and Rom 12:12, to name only a few.

In this chapter we're going to consider how to "keep it up" when it comes to prayer, or as the apostle Paul puts it: how to "pray continually" (1 Thess 5:16–18). The practice that will help us to do this is "developing a rhythm of prayer," and it seeks to integrate prayer into the fabric of our everyday lives. I think of it like a trellis supporting a vine, where our prayer life is the vine that we're seeking to grow upward toward God, and the trellis, or framework, is the rhythm of prayer that we develop, which provides structure and support to our prayers—enabling them to continue growing in the right direction. If we put our trellis in place, it should enable us to pray prayers of lament, compassionate release, and thankfulness, as well as creating times to embrace silence and to pray the Scriptures.

In this chapter there are four practical elements that we'll work through to develop a rhythm of prayer. Together they form a strong and sturdy trellis that, with God's grace and help, will withstand every situation that enters our lives. These elements are: finding a place to pray, choosing a pattern of prayer, adopting a posture as we pray, and beginning to allow prayer to permeate every aspect of our lives. My aim is to outline these four elements of "place," "pattern," "posture," and "permeate" in a way that provides principles that you can nuance with wisdom and grace for your own life. And while together they make up a supportive trellis, please know that the form these elements take in your life is completely adaptable and flexible. They can and should look different based upon your season and stage of life, as well as the make-up of your family, work, study, personality, and responsibilities.

Over time, this supporting trellis will help prayer to become a rhythm in your life. When I use the word "rhythm," I mean a repeated action that becomes like second nature as we practice it regularly. Rhythms are the subtle and almost unconscious movements that we make as we navigate life. We want to develop a rhythm of prayer that becomes like a reflex for us, helping us to pray continually regardless of our circumstances or season. We want prayer to sink down deep into our lives and infiltrate our very being, so that when the storms of life come, our default response is to pray. And while we're going to focus on how to do this when you're in a season of suffering or longing to pray for those in your lives who are enduring hardships, I believe this practice is one that's beneficial for followers of Jesus in all seasons of life. We all need a trellis to hold up our life of prayer, and developing a rhythm of prayer is how we put it into practice.

Find a Place to Pray

The first element in developing a rhythm of prayer is *finding a place to pray*. This element, along with choosing a pattern of prayer and posturing ourselves to pray, can be implemented in any order, but I've personally found that when I have a consistent place to pray I tend to become more regular in my prayer life.

It might sound strange to think about finding a particular place to pray; we can pray anywhere, right? While that's true, we saw Jesus model this in our third practice, "Embrace Silence," where he repeatedly went to a solitary place to pray. In the Sermon on the Mount, Jesus gives us greater insight into why this is so important. A crowd has gathered before Jesus, including his disciples, and he teaches them that they too should go to a specific place when they pray:

> And when you pray, do not be like the hypocrites, for they love to pray standing in the synagogues and on the street corners to be seen by others. Truly I tell you, they have received their reward in full. But when you pray, go into your room, close the door and pray to your Father, who is unseen. Then your Father, who sees what is done in secret, will reward you. (Matt 6:5–6)

Jesus is explicit here: God rewards those who spend time alone with him in prayer, their heavenly Father. Jesus even goes so far as to name a place—in your room with the door closed—as well as cautioning people against praying in a certain way—standing in religious buildings or to be seen by others.

Before we go any further, it's important to recognize two pieces of context in these verses that help us to avoid going too far off track. Firstly, there is a place for public prayer of course—Jesus is speaking here against the Pharisees and religious leaders of his day who prayed in order to be seen by other people. And secondly, when Jesus tells the crowd to go into their room and close the door to pray, he is *describing* the kind of prayer life that we should be cultivating, not *prescribing* the exact actions we must take.

The principle that Jesus is teaching us is this: finding a place to pray where we are alone, just us and our Father, is crucial to developing the life of prayer that we need and that God desires. Prayer is first and foremost between us and God, and Jesus recognizes that on a practical level we need to find a place to pray that is away from the distractions of life and the temptation to pray a certain way in front of other people. In a sense, Jesus is encouraging us to keep it simple, keep it real, and keep it up.

I first saw this modeled to me by one of the greatest pray-ers I know—my Dad. In the months after Rach had died, I just about threw in the towel on my faith. In many ways, I would have understood if Dad decided to give up on his faith as well. He was the one who found Rach after she collapsed, performed CPR on her before the ambulance arrived, and then grappled with the immeasurable grief of losing his daughter far too young. But instead of turning his back on Jesus, he doubled down on his faith by praying more than ever. Every morning for the next few years, he would rise before the sun and go up to a nearby mountain to pray. I'd wake up to the sound of his car arriving in the driveway, and if I ever asked him where he'd been, his response without fail was "up on the mountain with the Lord."

I know it wasn't always easy for him. There were countless mornings filled with tears and laments, questions and doubts. But no matter what his feelings were, he went to the same mountain every day to pray. There was every reason for Dad to grumble to others instead of going to God, or even to give up on praying because his suffering was so great. Instead, he found a place to pray, just him and his Father, and he went there each day. He took Jesus' example and teaching seriously, even in the depths of his despair.

I haven't had the heart yet to tell Dad that given his "mountain" is only sixty meters above sea level it would be better classified as a beachside headland—but that's beside the point. We all need to find our own "mountain" and go there regularly, no matter what comes our way in life. It might be a room where we can close our door behind us, a chair by the window where we won't be disturbed, the park bench down the road, or a morning walk where we can be alone with God. I've tried plenty of places over the years and have settled on an armchair at home, coffee in hand, and my Bible by my side.

It's also helpful to acknowledge that in one sense, the place doesn't matter as much as our willingness to go there regularly. There's no rule or requirement about finding a place and sticking to it for life. But I do find that having an established place to go and meet with God in prayer removes a barrier to praying as well. On days when I don't feel like praying, I don't need to think about where I'll go, I simply show up in the same location as the day before. It's one less thing to think about, and a way of helping myself to feel at peace and at home in the company of God when life might be throwing all kinds of curveballs my way.

I love the honest example of Pete Greig, the founder of the worldwide prayer movement 24-7 Prayer, who says that "after decades of night-and-day prayer, I have come to believe that 99 per cent of it is just showing up; making the effort to become consciously present to the God who is constantly present to us."[2]

If the work of "showing up" to pray is 99 percent of keeping up a rhythm of prayer, what better way to begin than by finding a place to pray today. Where might that place be for you?

2. Greig, *How to Pray*, 26.

Choose a Pattern of Prayer

The next element that we need to integrate into our rhythm of prayer is *choosing a pattern of prayer*. By "pattern" I'm talking about a consistent time each day when we come before God to pray. It could be first thing in the morning when you wake up, last thing before going to bed, on your commute to or from work, during your lunch break, or any other time throughout the day. In the final element, permeate, we'll even consider how to grow your pattern from one time to multiple times each day. Before we get to that step though, we need to recognize that while it's incredibly valuable to find a place to pray, it's unlikely that we'll ever develop a rhythm of prayer if we have no established pattern for when we will pray.

Whether we realize it or not, we thrive when we have habits in our lives. We all have habits that we lean on in every moment of the day. These habits determine things like the routine we go through every morning, the default responses we give to certain questions, our unconscious choice to reach for our phones when we're waiting in line, the way we carry out our work, as well as the decisions we make when it comes to our spiritual life in areas such as prayer. James Clear, the bestselling author of *Atomic Habits*, says that "habit formation is the process by which a behavior becomes progressively more automatic through repetition. The more you repeat an activity, the more the structure of your brain changes to become efficient at that activity."[3] This means that if we never choose a regular time to spend with God in prayer, it becomes very difficult to ever form a habit of prayer. On the flip side, "people who make a specific plan for when and where they will perform a new habit are more likely to follow through."[4]

What I'm trying to point out is that when we choose a place and a pattern for prayer, we give ourselves the best chance of following through on our intentions—regardless of whether any given day is full of joy or sorrow. Knowing the "when"—our pattern for prayer—and "where"—our place to pray—are crucial to

3. Clear, *Atomic Habits*, 143.
4. Clear, *Atomic Habits*, 70–71.

developing a deep and lasting rhythm of prayer in our lives. As we've seen in practice three, "Embrace Silence," this is something that was modeled in Jesus' own prayer life: "Jesus often withdrew to lonely places and prayed" (Luke 5:16). And while we don't have all the details of Jesus' schedule, we're graciously given enough details in the Gospels to know that Jesus would "often" find a place to pray that was away from people and the worries of life, and that his pattern was frequently to do this "early in the morning" (Mark 1:35).

This combination of having a regular time to pray along with an isolated space for prayer was clearly indispensable to the way that Jesus lived, and I'm convinced that it should be non-negotiable for us as well for at least three reasons. Firstly, having a pattern and place to pray positions us to spend time with God every day regardless of whether we want to or not. Pete Greig gives us a gentle caution for these times: "A Christian who prays only when they feel like it may survive but they will never thrive . . . because grace needs a little space to take root between the cracks of a person's life."[5] It's deeply human to have moments when praying is hard. But when we find a place to pray and commit to a pattern of praying in that location, we create space for grace to grow. Secondly, having a pattern and place for prayer shields us from the need to make practical choices when trials and hardship come our way. The best way to prepare for times of suffering is before they arrive, not during them, and when we've developed a pattern of prayer that is already ingrained in our daily lives, we stand in good stead to weather the storms of life that will inevitably come. And thirdly, when we have a pattern to our prayers it protects us from both the busyness of life and our own laziness, because it makes prayer our default position instead of prayerlessness. Prayer becomes harder to leave out the longer we practice it, because slowly but surely it becomes a source of oxygen amidst the breathlessness of life in our chaotic world.

On a practical level, there are no hard and fast rules for what time of day you should choose. I began by choosing to pray in the

5. Greig, *How to Pray*, 39.

morning because I'm more awake and alert then, and it's an opportunity to begin the day in prayer. I even set an alarm to remind me to pray each morning, which is a practice I know many people have found helpful. But there are plenty of people who choose to pray primarily in the evening or at other times throughout the day because it works better for them than the morning. The important part is to get it into your schedule and calendar and over time to allow it to sink down deep into your bones and your body as it becomes a habit in your life. Finally, I'd encourage you to start with a small amount of time if you're just beginning to develop a rhythm of prayer, even just two minutes. It might not feel like a lot to begin with—or it might feel like a lot!—but it's enough of a crack in the surface for God's grace to enter, take root, and grow.

Now it's over to you. When is the best time in your day to go to the place you've chosen and pray? What will your pattern of prayer be?

Adopt a Posture in Prayer

I grew up attending an Anglican church on Sydney's Northern Beaches, and later had the joy of spending seven years as part of the pastoral staff at the same church. For most of my time at this church, there had been a long-running and mostly friendly debate about removing the heavy wooden pews that filled our main auditorium and replacing them with more modern chairs. I was a big advocate for removing them because I couldn't see how they possibly appealed to anyone under the age of sixty. In my mind they scored a zero out of ten for comfort, a one out of ten for aesthetic appeal, and they were also a safety hazard because they had these weird little steps that folded down at the back and crowded the aisles. When I was making these points rather strongly to a more elderly member of the congregation, he asked me if I knew what the "steps" were for.

"For short people like me to stand on and see over the tall people?" I responded.

"No! They're for getting on your knees to pray and receive communion," he snapped back, partly in frustration, before a smile appeared as he realized how oblivious I was.

At that point I'd been on the staff team for all of four months. It was a humbling moment to say the least. Not so much because I was wrong; more so because I wasn't sure I'd ever thought to kneel before God in prayer. The worst part was, I'd glossed over the countless references to this in the Scriptures too: Jesus kneels before God and prays at the Mount of Olives before being arrested (Luke 22:41), Paul "kneels before the Father" to pray perhaps his most well-known prayer (Eph 3:14–21), and we're told that "every knee will bow" at the name of Jesus when he returns (Phil 2:9–11). It triggered a question in my mind: Does the posture we take with our bodies in prayer matter at all?

The third element of developing a rhythm of prayer is adopting a posture in prayer, and it flows directly from what I learned as I mulled over this question. In time I came to see that not only is kneeling prayer a practice that shows up countless times in Scripture, but it also has a long history amongst the people of God. It's a habit that has been passed down throughout church history and is still practiced by many churches today. Perhaps the most well-known example is James, the brother of Jesus and author of the epistle of James. The fourth-century historian Eusebius recounts this story about James:

> And he was in the habit of entering alone into the temple, and was frequently found upon his knees begging forgiveness for the people, so that his knees became hard like those of a camel, in consequence of his constantly bending them in his worship of God, and asking forgiveness for the people.[6]

For all his time in prayer, James ended up with the nickname "camel knees." I'm personally glad I've avoided that nickname, but it's certainly caused me to reconsider my own prayer life and the

---

6. Eusebius, *Ecclesiastical History*, bk. 2, ch. 23.

posture I take before God. And he's just one example of a long line of Christians who've chosen to pray on their knees.

The reason for kneeling to pray is that it is an embodied way of expressing humility before God. It shows the inward posture of our hearts through the outward positioning of our bodies. It doesn't magically make us pray differently or transform our hearts in an instant, but it is a physical reminder of the God to whom we pray. This is a vital addition to our rhythm of prayer because it keeps us focused on *who* we are praying to and not just *when* and *where* we are praying.

Again, there's no requirement or command in Scripture for this specific posture of prayer. But the premise of posturing ourselves physically in an intentional way when we pray is one that we'd all do well to recover. For me, I've found that the most helpful posture I can take isn't kneeling. Instead, I bow my head, close my eyes, and turn the open palms of my hands to face upward. Bowing my head is a physical act of reminding myself that I'm coming humbly before the God of the universe in prayer. Closing my eyes is a practical way of focusing my time, attention, and worship on God and not on what is around me. I'm easily distracted, so this allows me to devote this practice of prayer solely to God. And finally, I open my hands and turn my palms to face upwards as a tangible gesture that I am offering my whole life to God when I pray. This also helps me to remember to pray in a way that anticipates God's response to my prayers, and to be ready to receive those responses with thankfulness.

The purpose of this section has been to give you some examples of how you could physically position yourself to pray. You could kneel to pray, or you could bow your head, close your eyes, and bring your hands together. But perhaps going for a walk around the block, standing up, or lying down is more beneficial for you. There isn't a rule here, only some best practices that have been passed down throughout church history that teach us the value of adopting a consistent posture when we pray. Once you've found a place to pray and a pattern for our prayers, introducing this element might be helpful for adopting an inner heart posture of humility before God. What posture might be helpful for you to adopt in prayer?

Allow Prayer to Permeate Your Life

The fourth element that makes up a rhythm of prayer is allowing prayer to permeate your life. It's the movement from praying once per day to "praying continually," where you begin to look for other moments throughout the day to pray as it becomes the natural and default response of your heart to every circumstance that you face.

If we return to our image of the trellis and the vine from the start of this chapter, this element is how we reinforce our trellis and make it even stronger by guiding our prayer life multiple times each day as it grows upward toward God. My encouragement would be to only consider how prayer can permeate your life after you've established the first three elements, because they're the most foundational and crucial to flourishing in prayer. It's also important to recognize that developing a rhythm of prayer is not always as nice and neat as it might seem here. We can't and shouldn't orchestrate and plan every detail of our prayer life. We have a relationship with God that allows us access to his throne of grace at any time, in any place, and in any circumstance (Heb 4:16), and this always lies at the heart of prayer. Permeating our life with prayer is simply another practical step to allow prayer to occupy our entire lives and to allow prayer to flow intuitively in every moment of every day.

This recognition that prayer is a relationship is also what lies at the heart of the apostle Paul's persistent teaching on praying continually (Rom 12:12; 1 Thess 5:16–18; Phil 4:6; Eph 6:18; and Col 4:2). He recognizes the reality that we have unique circumstances such as jobs, families, and responsibilities that are good and God-given. Paul's assumption isn't that we'd give up all those things to pray 24/7, but rather that prayer would be on the tip of our tongue and the top of our mind in every situation, circumstance, and occasion. He wants our response to everything in life to be prayer, even in times of hardship and suffering. But the question is, how do we do that?

Well, like a person who desires to run a marathon one day, we start slowly—gradually going a little further each time. We incorporate prayer into more of our lives over time. I want to leave you with two practical ways of doing that to finish this practice of developing a rhythm of prayer.

Introduce a Second Time of Daily Prayer

The most logical step to begin praying more frequently is to introduce a second time of prayer each day. In fact, this practice has a long and rich history amongst God's people. Having considered the breadth of church history, Tim Keller suggests that "there seems to be unanimity from the Christian past in all its branches that we should turn our thoughts to God at set times more than once during a twenty-four-hour period."[7] We see this example as early as St. Benedict of Nursia, who in the fifth century encouraged believers to pray each hour.[8] This practice was perhaps slightly ambitious, and was made more manageable during the reformation, when Martin Luther began to advocate for the practice of praying twice daily as a minimum.[9] Follow Luther's lead, Thomas Cranmer developed the Book of Common Prayer with guided opportunities to pray in the morning and evening.[10]

It seems to be a relatively recent phenomenon to reduce our times of prayer to a single "quiet time" each day. The testimony of the church is punctuated by believers who were devoted to praying multiple times each day. If you feel like you've established a routine of praying once each day, then it's likely that the most helpful next step to grow your prayer life is introducing a second time of daily prayer. Framing the day in prayer in both the morning

7. Keller, *Prayer*, 24.
8. Hansen, *Kneeling with Giants*, 18.
9. Parrish, *Simple Way to Pray*, 28.
10. Jacobs, Book of Common Prayer, 24–27.

and evening is a time-honored way of implementing this practice, but like I've said before, there's no obligation to do this according to certain customs. The goal is to "pray continually," and this is another step in that process. The Book of Common Prayer, the Psalms, and other prayer books can be useful guides to help you get started too, as they offer some language for your journey into praying more regularly—especially when words may be difficult to come by in the hardest of times.

Mark Moments with Prayer

The second way of allowing prayer to permeate your days is by marking specific moments that occur regularly with prayer. By choosing to pray in moments that are already a habitual part of your day, like commuting to or from work, mealtimes, brushing your teeth, leaving the office, or putting the kids to bed, we provide ourselves with further opportunities to come before God in prayer.

Every day for several years, I would lay my hands briefly on my desk in our church office and commit all the people, tasks and worries of my day to God before I went home. It's marking moments like this throughout our days with prayer that embodies the spirit of Paul's encouragement. We all have these transitional moments every day; we just need to notice that they're opportunities to pray. It could be offering a prayer of thankfulness to God that He has sustained you through another day upon lying down each night, asking for strength and grace for the day each as you brush your teeth in the morning, requesting God's provision of healing and health for you or a friend before you eat a meal, lamenting the tragedies in our world immediately after you catch up on the news, or laying your hands on your desk at the end of a work day and committing the difficulties of your job into the Lord's hands while you rest from your work for the evening. By tying these moments of prayer to repeated transitions or actions throughout our days, we instinctively develop a healthy habit of prayerful dependence on God that defines our lives.

What if we began to see every moment of our days as opportunities for prayer, not obstacles to being present with God? And what if we persevered in this practice, refusing to be discouraged, instead remembering that as prayer permeates our lives, peace is on offer from Jesus in return?

The practice of developing a rhythm of prayer will take time, but putting this trellis in place to help you grow towards God in prayer is one of the most important commitments you'll make in your spiritual life. It positions you to come before God and pray in any and all of the ways that we've mentioned throughout this book, and to find peace in the process.

> May you have wisdom in finding a place to come before God in prayer,
> perseverance in the pattern that you choose,
> humility in the posture that you adopt,
> and grace to allow prayer to permeate your life.
> And may it all result in glory, honor and praise to Jesus,
> In his name,
> Amen.

Epilogue

Finding Peace through Prayer

As I SIT HERE, twelve years after the storm hit and shook my life to its core, the weather remains a little cloudy. While I can see the sunshine streaming through the clouds because of the unshakable peace that I possess in Christ Jesus, I still long for the day when the sun is all I see. A day when my body and mind will be renewed, and I'll stand in the presence of God with Rach and every loved one I've lost who knows Jesus.

The truth is, the process of finding peace through prayer is not always linear, and it may not come to completion in this life either. It ebbs and flows, sometimes feeling like we're taking one step forward and two steps back. And yet slowly but surely as we persevere in prayer, our peace increases by the grace of God. Peace doesn't always come in an instant, rather over time and across seasons as we continue to cling to Christ Jesus.

It's taken me a long time, but I've learned to place my unwavering trust in the words of Scripture, knowing that when I come before God in prayer, he will guard my heart and mind in Jesus with an otherworldly peace (Phil 4:6–7). My earnest prayer as you finish this book is that you will also have a deeper and more resolute faith in this truth, no matter what hardships come your way in life. To that end, I want to leave you with these brief encouragements for finding peace through prayer.

Put the Practices into Practice

The apostle Paul tells us in Philippians 4:6: "Do not be anxious about anything, but in every situation, by prayer and petition, with thanksgiving, present your requests to God." Paul envisages prayer making a difference to how we live in every moment. And it begins with making a deliberate choice to turn from feeling anxious and uncertain about our hardships and toward Jesus as we take up a life of active and intentional prayer.

After reading this book, it would be a shame for your prayer life to remain unchanged. You've put in the time and energy to read this far, but the benefit really begins when you make the choice to practice praying for yourself. Before you put this book down, I want to encourage you to form a plan for how you can put some of the practices we've learned into action in your life. Feel free to begin small, taking one or two of the practices and working them into your days—perhaps as part of your regular rhythm of prayer. It doesn't matter which practices you chose, rather that you know how and when you're going to practice them. Over time, you can begin to incorporate further practices as you feel led. And in return, God promises that you will receive peace in Christ Jesus. Take a moment now and consider how you can put these practices into practice in your life.

Remember It's about Jesus

It may sound strange to conclude a book on prayer by saying this, but I actually hope you take away something greater than just a desire to pray more: a deeper love for Jesus. While prayer is often the means through which God mediates his peace to us, Paul tells us that this peace is ultimately found in our Savior: "And the peace of

God, which transcends all understanding, will guard your hearts and your minds in Christ Jesus" (Phil 4:7).

Jesus is the one who makes peace possible: keep your eyes fixed on him. There is immense value in learning practices for prayer, but they are always a means to an end, and the end is knowing, loving, and being with Jesus, the Prince of Peace. Remain close to him by continuing to pursue a purposeful life of prayer in the middle of your pain, and keep praying for those you care about who face hardships of every kind. And as you pray, remember that the life, death, and resurrection of Jesus is what guards your heart and mind with a peace that surpasses comprehension, no matter the circumstances that you face.

Look toward Your Final Dwelling Place

Finally, keep looking to how your story will end. Right now, our lives might be marked by hardship, sorrows, disappointment, and pain. But one day, this will all be undone when a new creation arrives and sin, suffering, and death are no more. This is the vision that John records for us in Revelation 21:

> Then I saw "a new heaven and a new earth," for the first heaven and the first earth had passed away, and there was no longer any sea. I saw the Holy City, the new Jerusalem, coming down out of heaven from God, prepared as a bride beautifully dressed for her husband. And I heard a loud voice from the throne saying, "Look! God's dwelling place is now among the people, and he will dwell with them. They will be his people, and God himself will be with them and be their God. 'He will wipe every tear from their eyes. There will be no more death' or mourning or crying or pain, for the old order of things has passed away." (Rev 21:1–4)

How beautiful will that day be? We will dwell with God, and death, mourning, crying and pain will all be banished forever. Every ounce of suffering we face now will be finished.

Epilogue

I especially love the image of God wiping tears from our eyes, because it shows us that he knows that our tears will still be there on that final day. God is not offended by their presence, because he anticipates catching them as they roll down our cheeks—and promises to make sure that they will never flow again. This is why we continue to grieve and lament, cry and pray, mourn and petition—because we're longing for this time to come, when we meet God face to face.

While you wait, keep praying, and know that there is a glorious day on the horizon when you will finally dwell with God and receive an everlasting peace that will never be taken from you.

> May you not be anxious about anything,
> but in every situation, by prayer and petition,
> and with thanksgiving,
> present your requests to God.
> And may the peace of God,
> which transcends all understanding,
> guard your heart and mind in Christ Jesus.
> In Jesus' name,
> Amen.

Bibliography

Augustine. *Exposition of the Psalms 121–150*. Exposition of the Psalms 5. New York: New City, 2014.

Barker, Kit. "Lament as Divine Discourse: God's Voice in Our Cry." In *Finding Lost Words: The Church's Right to Lament*, edited by G. Geoffrey Harper and Kit Barker, 55–65. Eugene, OR: Wipf & Stock, 2017.

Bonhoeffer, Dietrich. *Life Together*. New York: Harper & Row, 1954.

Brother Lawrence. *The Practice of the Presence of God*. Mineola, NY: Dover, 2005.

"Cameron." https://babynames.com/name/Cameron.

"Campbell." https://babynames.com/name/Campbell.

Clear, James. *Atomic Habits: An Easy and Proven Way to Build Good Habits and Break Bad Ones*. London: Penguin Random House, 2018.

Collins, Gail, and Bret Stephens. "'There Are Almost Too Many Things to Worry About.'" *New York Times*, Mar 14, 2022. https://www.nytimes.com/2022/03/14/opinion/putin-biden-cuomo-texas.html.

Comer, John Mark. *The Ruthless Elimination of Hurry: How to Stay Emotionally Healthy and Spiritually Alive in the Chaos of the Modern World*. Colorado Springs: Waterbrook, 2019.

"Compassion Fatigue: Signs, Symptoms, and How to Cope." Canadian Medical Association, Dec 8, 2020. https://www.cma.ca/physician-wellness-hub/content/compassion-fatigue.

Crowe, Dustin. *The Grumbler's Guide to Giving Thanks: Reclaiming the Gifts of a Lost Spiritual Discipline*. Chicago: Moody, 2020.

Eland, Edwin. *The Layman's Guide to the Book of Common Prayer*. London: Longmans, Green & Co., 1896.

Bibliography

Eldredge, John. *Get Your Life Back: Everyday Practices for a World Gone Mad.* Nashville: Nelson, 2020.

Eusebius. *Ecclesiastical History: Complete and Unabridged.* Translated by Christian Frederic Crusé. Peabody, MA: Hendrickson, 2006.

Gleddiesmith, Stacey. "My God, My God, Why? Understanding the Lament Psalms." Jun 2010. https://www.reformedworship.org/article/june-2010/my-god-my-god-why.

Goldsworthy, Graeme. *Prayer and the Knowledge of God: What the Whole Bible Teaches.* Downers Grove: InterVarsity, 2004.

Greig, Pete. *How to Pray: A Simple Guide for Normal People.* London: Hodder & Stoughton, 2019.

Guthrie, Nancy. *I'm Praying for You: 40 Days of Praying the Bible for Someone Who Is Suffering.* Leyland, UK: 10Publishing, 2021.

Hansen, Gary Neal. *Kneeling with Giants: Learning to Pray with History's Best Teachers.* Downers Grove: InterVarsity, 2012.

Hansen, G. Walter. *The Letter to the Philippians.* The Pillar New Testament Commentary. Grand Rapids: Eerdmans, 2009.

Harper, G. Geoffrey. "Lament and the Sovereignty of God: Theological Reflections on Psalm 88." In *Finding Lost Words: The Church's Right to Lament,* edited by G. Geoffrey Harper and Kit Barker, 80–93. Eugene, OR: Wipf & Stock, 2017.

Harrison Warren, Tish. *Prayer in the Night: For Those Who Work or Watch or Weep.* Downers Grove: InterVarsity, 2021

Hatchett, Marion. *Commentary on the American Prayer Book.* New York: Harper Collins, 1995.

Hibbs, Pierce Taylor. *Finding Hope in Hard Things: A Positive Take on Suffering.* N.p.: Pierce Taylor Hibbs, 2020.

"'It Is Well With My Soul'—Spafford Hymn." Kosinki Trust. https://www.spaffordhymn.com/.

Jacobs, Alan. *The Book of Common Prayer: A Biography,* Princeton: Princeton University Press, 2013.

Kaiser, Walter C., Jr. "The Laments of Lamentation Compared to the Psalter." In *The Psalms: Language for All Seasons of the Soul,* edited by Andrew J. Schmutzer and David M. Howard Jr., 127–35. Chicago: Moody, 2013.

Kapic, M. Kelly. *You're Only Human: How Your Limits Reflect God's Design and Why That's Good News.* Grand Rapids: Brazos, 2022.

Keller, Timothy. *Prayer: Experiencing Awe and Intimacy with God.* London: Hodder & Stoughton, 2014.

"Kennedy." https://babynames.com/name/Kennedy.

Lewis, C. S. *The Magician's Nephew.* London: HarperCollins, 1955.

Longman, Tremper, III. "From Weeping to Rejoicing: Psalm 150 as the Conclusion to the Psalter." In *The Psalms: Language for All Seasons of the Soul,* edited by Andrew J. Schmutzer and David M. Howard Jr., 219–30. Chicago: Moody, 2013.

Bibliography

Miller, Paul E. *A Praying Life: Connecting with God in a Distracting World.* Colorado Springs: NavPress, 2009.

Naftulin, Julia. "Here's How Many Times We Touch Our Phones Every Day." *Business Insider,* July 13, 2016. https://www.businessinsider.com/dscout-research-people-touch-cell-phones-2617-times-a-day-2016-17.

"An Order for Compline." The Church Hymnal Corporation. https://www.bcponline.org/DailyOffice/compline.html.

"An Order for Night Prayer." The Church of England. https://www.churchofengland.org/prayer-and-worship/worship-texts-and-resources/common-worship/daily-prayer/night-prayer-compline.

Parrish, Archie. *A Simple Way to Pray: The Wisdom of Martin Luther on Prayer.* Marietta, GA: Serve International, 2009.

Pascal, Blaise. *Pensées.* Translated by A. J. Krailsheimer. Westminster, MD: Penguin, 2013.

Patston, Kirk R. "Lament and Pastoral Care." In *Finding Lost Words: The Church's Right to Lament,* edited by G. Geoffrey Harper and Kit Barker, 237–48. Eugene, OR: Wipf & Stock, 2017.

Paul, Kari. "Millennials Waste Five Hours a Day Doing This One Thing." *New York Post,* May 18, 2017. https://nypost.com/2017/05/18/millennials-waste-five-hours-a-day-doing-this-one-thing/.

Peterson, Eugene. *Answering God: The Psalms as Tools for Prayer.* San Francisco: HarperCollins, 1991.

Petersen, Randy. *Be Still My Soul: The Inspiring Stories behind 175 of the Most-Loved Hymns.* Carol Stream, IL: Tyndale House, 2014.

"Portia." https://babynames.com/name/Portia.

Sherill, A. J. *Being with God: The Absurdity, Necessity, and Neurology of Contemplative Prayer.* Grand Rapids, MI: Brazos, 2021.

Sittser, Gerald. *Water from a Deep Well: Christian Spirituality from Early Martyrs to Modern Missionaries.* Downers Grove: InterVarsity, 2007.

Spurgeon, C. H. *The Practice of Praise.* Springdale, PA: Whitaker House, 1995.

Sullivan, Andrew. "I Used to Be a Human Being." *New York Magazine,* Sep, 2016. http://nymag.com/intelligencer/2016/09/andrew-sullivan-my-distraction-sickness-and-yours.html.

"Understanding the Meaning of Compassion." Compassion International. https://www.compassion.com/child-development/meaning-of-compassion/.

Villodas, Rich. *The Deeply Formed Life: Five Transformative Values to Root Us in the Way of Jesus.* Colorado Springs: Waterbrook, 2020.

Vroegop, Mark. *Dark Clouds, Deep Mercy: Discovering the Grace of Lament.* Wheaton, IL: Crossway, 2019.

Wolterstorff, Nicholas. *Lament for a Son.* Grand Rapids: Eerdmans, 1987.